CW01507246

A COLD FINGER CAME DOWN FROM ABOVE

War, espionage and spying on the spies from within

Eleanor Fane

I dedicate this book to my mother Pamela
and to my children Anna and Tom

© Eleanor Fane.

All rights reserved. Apart from any use permitted under UK copyright law no part of this publication may be reproduced, stored in a retrieval system, or transmitted in any form or by any means without the prior written permission of the publisher, nor be otherwise circulated in any form of binding or cover other than that in which it is published and without a similar condition being imposed on the subsequent Purchaser.

ISBN: 978-1-916722-21-7

Design and layout   Tim Underwood
Printed by Sarsen Press, 22 Hyde Street, Winchester, Hampshire SO23 7DR

Contents

Introduction

"**N**EVER disclose anything over the telephone!" My mother Pamela, thinking she had overheard an indiscretion on the phone, swept into the room to stop me in my tracks, and then swept out again with as much speed and gusto as she had entered. Once she was out of earshot, my friend and I put her outburst down to her somewhat theatrical character. What we did not know was that she had spent nearly 25 years working for British Intelligence. She joined the service aged 18 at the beginning of the Second World War and continued until she was 41 in 1964 when she retired to start a family and get married.

Her job initially involved surveillance and censorship in London, Bermuda and finally Cairo in Egypt where she worked for 18 months until the end of the war when she was mentioned in despatches by the Commander in Chief, Middle East Forces, for her outstandingly good service.

On her return to London in 1945 she began working for the Home Office and in 1950 she joined MI5.

At the height of the Cold War during the '50s, her work increasingly involved surveillance of some of her colleagues in MI5. She had been part of a phone tapping team interested in nine suspected Soviet spies working inside British Intelligence including Guy Burgess, Anthony Blunt, Donald Maclean and Kim Philby. No surprise, therefore, that she was anxious about us ever saying anything indiscreet over the telephone.

All officers in the service, including my mother, were forbidden under the Official Secrets Act to speak of what they did. Now, thanks to the Freedom of Information Act, documents have become accessible which throw new light on the world of intelligence of which she was a part. Until now it had not been possible to find out that she was involved in attempts to prevent the defection of Guy Burgess and Donald Maclean to Soviet Russia or her contribution to attempting to unravel the mystery surrounding the death of Commander Crabb, a naval diver, in Portsmouth Harbour in 1956. The death of Crabb to this day remains shrouded in much secrecy.

In 1964 she retired, and married my father Charles Fane two years later. They bought a manor house in the Hampshire countryside where they raised three daughters of whom I was the eldest. During those years the manor was full of a wonderfully eclectic mix of farm workers, villagers, vicars, shooting parties, earls and dukes, all of whom were welcomed with the same vigorous hospitality.

Despite our attempts to persuade her to do so, my mother never spoke about her work until the 1980s when, dying of breast cancer, she met Chapman Pincher, a Daily Express journalist and expert on espionage, who also wrote books on Soviet spies working undercover in British Intelligence. She told him that whenever she had tried to uncover suspected spies "a cold finger came down from above," and further action was blocked. Specifically she was referring to attempts, after months of research by MI5 surveillance officers, of which she was one, to get their superiors to stop the defections of Guy Burgess and Donald Maclean to Soviet Russia in 1951. They failed.

During the 1970s I became curious about our mother's secret past. I would try to ask her about her intelligence work but she refused to tell me anything, using phrases like, "I will go to prison if I talk". At this point in time, she was relishing her role as lady of the manor and had, in no time, taken all the ladies of the village under her charge. The thought of her being dragged off and away from this world in the back of a Black Mariah seemed preposterous. She certainly would not have gone without putting up a fight. It did alarm me sufficiently, however, not to pursue the subject further. I knew nothing about the things she had witnessed, seen or done but there was a palpable aura of fear in her voice when approached on the subject, a sense of burden and too many years of secrets taking their toll. There was also the feeling that my mother was terribly alone with her unspeakable past. Long, life-changing years, suppressed by a wall of silence and shrouded by mystery.

Although my mother did not talk about her work there were things she did that were, with hindsight, a bit unusual. Her fear of phone tapping was evident and small clues of training decades ago that gave her unusual skills were occasionally revealed. On one occasion when my mother took my sisters and me for a walk she, without warning, started running towards a rather high locked gate. She was in her early sixties at the time. We looked at each other in alarm as she got closer to the gate. She picked up speed and then effortlessly vaulted over it. Clearly a useful skill if you are running away from an enemy in the countryside.

Sometimes her friend Sheila Jaimeson would come to stay with us. We knew she had been 'a spy' with my mother. When they used to walk round the garden my best friend and I would climb onto the roof of a cow shed and prostrate ourselves on the roof in order to spy on *them*. We never heard anything but thought we were terribly clever and daring especially as, in order to get down we had to jump off the roof into where the cows were and try not to slip on the cow poo.

Sheila was frightened of mice. On one occasion I strode into the drawing room dangling a live mouse by its tail, Sheila shrieked and leapt onto the sofa. I pondered over the fact that my mother's spy friend must have been brave during her time in intelligence and yet could be, so easily, undone by a mouse.

My mother's domestic life seemed chaotic and hectic but her filing cabinet revealed skills probably learnt from years of filing for the service. Even her Christmas card list was filed alphabetically with a separate list of who she had forgotten and who had forgotten her.

Meeting places were referred to as 'Checkpoint Charlie.' It was not until the Berlin Wall came down in 1989 that I realised that there was a real 'Checkpoint Charlie' in the Berlin Wall.

Contemplating the leap.

The mother I remember was noisy and colourful, always doing ten things at once and the person that everyone invited to their party because they knew that the minute she entered the room the party would liven up. Her driving was unnerving, she never understood the gears of a car. Often she would stop at a traffic light and when it went green there would be a frantic grappling with the gear stick and once she had found a gear, usually 4th, she would put her foot down hard on the accelerator and painfully slowly lurch forward or stall. She proudly announced that she had never had a driving test as she had learnt to drive during the war and amazingly she continued to drive without being tested all her life. The locals knew to give her a wide berth when they saw her coming. My father on the other hand drove at a frightening speed in a car so filled with cigarette smoke you could barely see out of the window.

When my friends came to stay they were drawn to my mother like a magnet. She always managed to make them laugh.

My mother died in 1987 but it was only shortly before her death that she mentioned her work to me. "I feel that my entire career was a waste of time as all my bosses were spies." This was in relation to the death in 1983 of Anthony Blunt, a former MI5 Officer. The ensuing press articles named him a Soviet spy. In the '50s he was well known to my mother as she was part of a phone tapping team monitoring his conversations as he was on a list of nine suspected Soviet spies working at the time for the British Intelligence Services. She knew, however, that the work she and countless others did in extreme conditions for many years contributed to the freedom we enjoy today.

This is an account of a courageous and colourful life lived to the full, often in extreme conditions, during the madness of the Second World War and the Cold War.

Research – Harry Chapman Pincher

It was the 1970s. My sisters and I on returning from boarding school, usually starving, would head out into the shed to see if there was any promising food in the freezer. Every once in a while there would be a frozen trout eyeballing us from inside. We would look at each other and one of us would say "that spy man has been to see Mummy again." The man in question was Harry Chapman Pincher, an investigative reporter and a passionate fisherman, who had spent sixty years researching Soviet spying against Great Britain and the United States and written a number of books on the subject of Soviet spies working undercover in British Intelligence. He visited my mother on several occasions to try to get information from her on Soviet agents planted by Russia in MI5 and MI6 in the 1930's. In the 1980s my mother was dying of breast cancer and wanted to tell Pincher about things with which she had been involved. He was the only person she spoke to about her involvement in two events. The rest she silently took to her grave. In his early books he referred to her as 'my source in MI5'[1] but in his final book, *Treachery: Betrayals, Blunders and Cover-ups: Six Decades of Espionage Against America and Great Britain*, published in America in 2009 shortly before his own death, he felt safe to mention her by name.

Years after my mother's death and frustrated with knowing nothing about her work except that she had spoken with Pincher on several occasions about her time in MI5, I decided to go through her old address book. There was his number and address. I just had to pluck up the courage to call him out of the blue to see if he would see me and give me some leads.

The first time I called him, and indeed each time I called him thereafter, he was charming and managed to fit me in for visits to his house between fishing trips and book writing. The first time I visited him I nervously banged on his front door to be greeted by his wife Billee, who exclaimed, "Oh, you have your mother's eyes!" Pincher welcomed me into their home and after a few minutes of polite chat about fishing, he proceeded to take me on a breathless journey of 20th century espionage and intelligence stories. He allowed me to record the whole conversation apart from the odd moment of saying "turn that thing off". Then he would tell me something not for the record and once he had finished he would say, "You can turn that thing on again". He was fairly certain that he was being listened in on so it seemed a futile gesture and I was not well informed enough to understand what he was talking about.

He told me that he had quoted my mother in several of his books but that she would not allow him to mention her by name. By giving me every page of every book that he had mentioned her in, he gave me enough material to go to the national archives and start my research. For Pincher it was frustrating that just as he was heading towards the end of his life, the Freedom of Information Act gave him access to documents, previously unavailable, which shed light on much of what he had been trying to prove, which was who were really Soviet agents working undercover in our Intelligence Services during the Second World War and the Cold War. Pincher seized on the material coming out of both British and Soviet archives, and said he paid his grandson to go to the National Archives and dig around for him.

In the context of him interviewing my mother he said that he much preferred to interview men: "You see, it is what I call the peacock factor, men love to tell you of their adventures whereas women would tend to say, 'I couldn't possibly discuss my job.'" The time that he had the most success in getting my mother to talk was after Anthony Blunt had been exposed. My mother was angry that he had not been exposed years earlier when she and her colleagues were trying to close the net and listened in to his calls. During the 1950s my mother's boss was Roger Hollis, head of MI5. Pincher was convinced that Hollis was the ultimate super spy for the Soviets and my mother's experience reinforced this conviction. She complained to Pincher that whenever she tried to get anywhere it was stopped from above and for much of her time in the Service Hollis was her boss. Whether Hollis was a spy or not was an area that Pincher and my mother wanted to discuss. Perhaps because my mother was terminally ill and time had passed she felt she could tell Pincher some of what she was involved in and be heard for the first and last time on the subject.

I did not start my research until years after her death and did not think I would get very far but after a couple of interviews with Pincher I had enough to get started. I did not expect to hear from him again, he was in his 90s by this stage but still pursuing material for his books.

The last interaction I had with him was when he wrote me a letter in June 2009. It opened with "Dear Eleanor, Greetings from a very old codger (95 not out)!"

Pincher was considered to be a controversial person both by the Intelligence Service and political leaders. A colleague of my mother's who worked in MI6 said that he put lives at risk by exposing agents in the field. But one could put the case that he helped to expose enemies from within. They also put lives at risk and indeed were the cause of many deaths not only of agents but also of their families who were often killed with them.

On 22nd February 2018 a snowstorm hit the UK called the 'Beast from the East'. London was in chaos. During this time a girlfriend and I trudged through the snow to the National Archives. As we were approaching the building the friend said, "You realise the Siberian storm is your fault, the Russians know you are researching and are trying to stop you!" Despite the storm we found some of what we were looking for and headed home to discuss and write.

A COLD FINGER CAME DOWN FROM ABOVE

16 Church Street,

01488 658397

Kintbury,

June 26, 2009

Berks RG17 9TR

Dear Elena

Greetings from a very old codger (95 not out)! You will recall that we talked some time ago about your mother's service in MI5. I write to let you know that I am about to celebrate my decrepitude by publishing a large book. Its title is 'TREACHERY – Betrayals, Blunders and Cover-ups : Six Decades of Espionage Against America and Great Britain' – and it is about to appear in the United States on 7 July. Your mother's counter-espionage activities get due mention.

It is, essentially, an account of my sixty years' investigative experiences in the intelligence and defence fields and contains a mass of new material culled from the National Archives and from Russian sources resulting in the exposure of many scandals. The appalling extent of treachery committed by so many British traitors has shocked even me . The dimensions of the military treachery, with naval consequences, are astounding. The 'authorities' here are not going to like it and I expect the usual rumpus.

I am publishing first in the US because I was, effectively, invited to do so by Robert Bernstein, the father figure of Random House, my American publisher. It was an invitation I could not refuse. I do not know when, or even if, it will be published here. So, should you like to acquire a copy the simplest way would be from Amazon on line, where it is already shown in all its glory listed at a reduced price with free delivery to the UK on or around July 7. Should you read it I would be grateful for your views. Anyway, it has given me the excuse to write to you.

Sadly, my wife, Billee (now 90) is crippled with knee problems and we have both given up driving. However we soldier on. I am grateful that I still have an intact memory.

Warmest wishes,

Chapman Pincher

A combination of passports, photographs, letters and interviews make for a vivid and colourful biography. During her teenage years she spent time in Buckingham Palace as a girl guide with the royal princesses, followed by evacuation to America where great aunts tried to sign her up as a debutante. My mother joined the Service at the outbreak of the Second World War, aged 18, and was sent to Bermuda to work as a censor, then later to Egypt where she was mentioned in despatches. During her time there she wrote letters to her parents which set a scene of long night shifts, illness and her boss having a nervous breakdown. She was spirited away leaving my mother in charge of 15 weeping women whilst simultaneously having to deal with a tragic houseboat disaster where the houseboat sank and a young man drowned saving the life of one of her work colleagues.

My mother's time in MI5 had a lasting effect on her. The betrayals and mistakes of her MI5 colleagues and bosses left her shocked and saddened. She later told Pincher that she knew that the British Intelligence officer Guy Burgess was a suspected Russian spy before he defected despite MI5 saying that he had not been a suspect. She was also working in MI5 the night before Buster Crabb dived under a boat bringing Kruschev to Britain on a peaceful visit. Crabb dived under the ship to examine it and was never seen again. MI5 said at the time that it had not known that Crabb would dive, but my mother said that her boss, Malcolm Cummings, told her that night that Crabb was going to dive and said that Cummings "was excited like a school boy."

For years my mother had to keep silent knowing that what the media were fed was sometimes not true to her experience working for MI5. She knew for years that Anthony Blunt, an MI5 officer and Surveyor of the Queen's Pictures, was a spy but it was not until Margaret Thatcher exposed him in 1979 that the public were made aware. She was frustrated and angry that the institution she had devoted her working life to had through many catastrophic errors let Soviet spies turn the institution, government, the CIA and MI6 upside down. It also seriously damaged our relationship with America which had trusted the British agents we sent them. However some of these agents were really working for the Russians, and this was at the time of the development of the atomic bomb.

My research has been a frustrating game of both waiting for enough time to go by so that documents can be released and Secret Service people dare to speak, and of finding that because of the wait, many of my mother's colleagues and bosses have died or are suffering from dementia. For example, I rang the husband of my mother's close friend and colleague, Sheila Jaimeson. She and my mother had worked and lived together in Egypt and had worked together in London after the war. Her husband said that he had burnt everything that she had kept from that time, and then told me she was in hospital with dementia and proceeded to tell me about his career in MI6. I imagine this was 'the peacock factor' that Pincher alluded to. In the 90s and up to about 2005 there were more dead ends than leads. The turning point was slow and labour intensive. My starting point was my mother's passport. It had a photograph of her as an 18 year old girl with the profession title, 'Government Official'. Inside the passport were all the visas to Bermuda, Egypt, Canada and America, and handwritten permission from Governors General giving her the right to travel to 'All countries in Europe including the Union of Soviet Socialist Republics and Turkey'. My first step was to map out what countries she was in when and then research what the Intelligence Services were doing in those countries at the time. After a bit of detective work I began to map out her extraordinary career made possible by 20th century world politics and war.

CHAPTER 1
Family Background

My mother's name was Pamela, her father was Captain Robert Millington Synge, his father was Anglo Irish and his mother was American. Robert was educated at Eton College followed by Trinity College Oxford from 1912-1914. He finished at Oxford as World War 1 was beginning and became an officer in the Coldstream Guards. Robert was twice wounded during the war but continued to serve throughout World War 1. During World War 2 and the Cold War he worked for the Foreign Office.

R.M.S. second row seated 5 from the right.

Robert 8th from right.

In 1921 Robert Synge was awarded a decoration conferred by His Majesty the Emperor of Japan, 'The Order of the Rising Sun', which was awarded for long and /or meritorious military service internationally.

In July 1922 he married my grandmother Christabel Etrenne Liddell. They had three children, the eldest of whom was my mother, Pamela born in 1923, Allen born 1930 and Gillian born in 1933.

After the First World War Robert worked for British Intelligence both in MI5 and MI6. At that time it was not unusual to recommend family members into the service, there was a 'keep it in the family' sort of mentality particularly if the family was aristocratic and their daughters were debutantes. Thus, years later at the age of 18, my mother Pamela was swiftly employed. Perhaps less flatteringly, according to her, the inhouse joke at the time was, if one had a particularly dim son the cry would be "send him to work in British Intelligence!"

After the First World War Robert worked in the Foreign Office in King Charles Street. His son, Allen Synge, recalled that in December 1939 the Foreign Secretary, Lord Halifax fired the whole department because Robert had suggested they all play a game of cricket in the corridors of the Foreign Office building and whilst in the middle of the game, a Foreign Office cipher clerk called Captain John King, was able to pick up an important phone call that he should not have been able to get to. It turned out that between 1935 and 1937 King had been secretly providing British

Foreign Office communications to the Russians. Once discovered he was sentenced in October 1939 to 10 years in prison as a spy. On the day that my grandfather and his colleagues were fired Robert invited them all to his house, which his son Allen in *The Talking book*[2] recalled "a grim memory of an unusual number of bowler hats parked in the hall at home as their owners debated their future."

After having been fired my grandfather was moved to the MI6 transport department where he arranged flights for other agents; this was a demotion both financially and career wise. On the arrest of King, my grandfather's pension was cut, he was re-employed on and off but was, according to his son Allen, "left with half a lifetime of anxiety."

In 1939 my grandfather was sent to Bletchley Park to work in decoding and then, shortly afterwards, went on to Cheltenham to work at the Government Code & Cypher School, which became GCHQ in 1946. He made a record of his wartime experiences and some of his writing can be found in the Imperial War Museum in London and the National Archives in Kew.

Christabel Liddell was born in 1897. She was one of four sisters, and a first cousin once removed to Alice Liddell who was the inspiration for Lewis Carroll's book *Alice in Wonderland*. Her father was Charles Lyon Liddell and her mother was Margaret Gresham Leveson-Gower, a distant cousin of the Queen Mother, Elizabeth Bowes-Lyon.

At the outbreak of World War I, Christabel was 17 years old. Keen to do her part, she joined the Voluntary Aid Detachment of War Service with the British Red Cross Society, which she remained in from March 1915 – March 1917. The Volunteers (VADs), had to be 18 years old so she lied about her age in order to be accepted. The VADs were made up of a voluntary unit of civilians to provide nursing care for military personnel both at home and overseas during both World War I and World War II. Most VAD's were middle and upper class girls who had no experience of hardship or suffering and they were ill-equipped to cope with the horror of front line battle hospitals often in foreign lands. My grandmother's training was undertaken in the Monastery Hospital in Rye where she learnt general nursing skills and attended a course of lectures and demonstrations of first aid in chemical warfare. She was then sent to work in a field hospital in Belgium until being sent home in May 1919 on grounds of ill health. On 12th May 1919 from ARMEE BELGE – SERVICE DE SANTE a Dr Marchelin confirmed that Miss Ch. Liddell, nurse at the Bonsecours Hospital, had to leave service due to ill health. Despite this, she was later decorated for distinguished service and was awarded the Red Cross Society's War Service Medal.

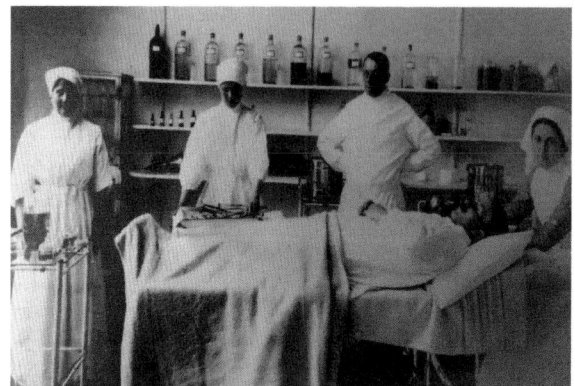

Christabel in her VAD uniform.

During her time as a VAD in Belgium my grandmother fell in love with an officer who was killed in battle shortly after they met. She was deeply saddened by this and mentioned it years later. However she later met my grandfather Captain Robert Synge with whom she enjoyed many years of love, family life and happiness.

In a conversation a few weeks before she died at the age of 94, she said to me, "You know dearest, I really am terribly lucky, in my lifetime I have seen horse and cart, the invention of airplanes, man traveling to the moon. More has been achieved by man in my lifetime than in the last thousand years". It was comforting to think that she felt so much had been achieved for the good in the 20th century despite two World Wars and the Cold War.

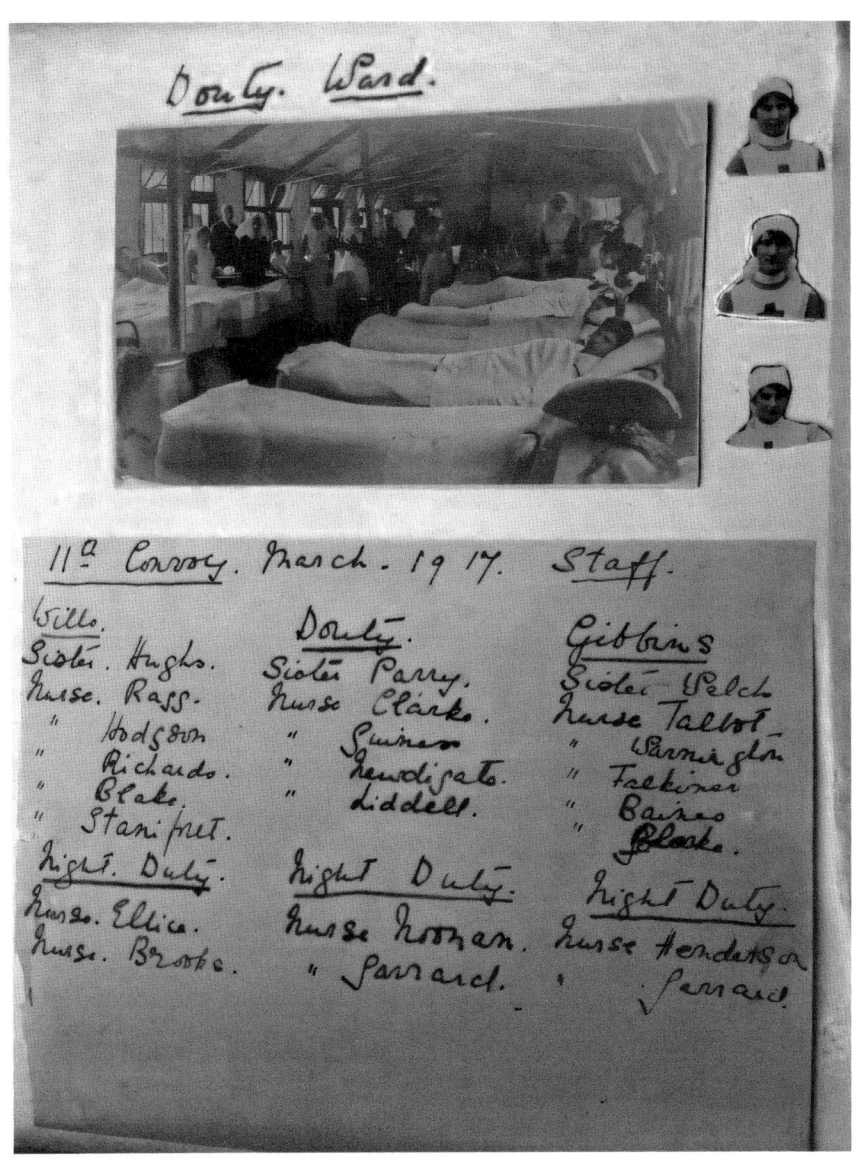

Staff shifts.

My mother Pamela was born in 1923, and grew up in Chorleywood in Hertfordshire. She had two younger siblings, Allen and Gillian. During her early years she was taught by a governess then she went to a local Parents National Education Union School, followed by Belstead House School, near Ipswich. Belstead, founded by Mrs Dudley Hervey in 1906, initially had a total of seven girls to educate but the school quickly became popular and the number of pupils grew. It wasn't long before Belstead was considered one of the best girls' schools in the country. Included in the curriculum were Domestic Science, Dairy, Poultry and Horticulture. The pupils were expected to have a firm understanding of French and music by the time the school had finished with them as these subjects were considered as important as giving the girls the core subjects needed to get them to university.[3]

CHAPTER 2

Royal Girl Guides

Royal Guides 1st Buckingham Palace Company

In 1937 whilst she was still at Belstead school, my mother's aunt Violet Synge was the Guide Commissioner for England and had been awarded the Silver Fish Award, the highest award in Girl Guiding. It had been decided by the royal family that their daughter, the 11 year old Princess Elizabeth, would benefit from mixing with girls of her own age and would benefit from being a Girl Guide. Violet was a spinster, hearty, strong and to some people slightly formidable. My mother, on the other hand, adored her aunt and found her charismatic and fun. It was decided that my mother would become one of 14 Girl Guides in the new Royal Guides pack.

Violet was first approached by the royal household's nanny, 'Crawfie', who asked her to set up and run a Girl Guide company for Princess Elizabeth at Buckingham Palace. Initially Violet said that guiding would not be appropriate at all for the royal Princess and tried to politely decline but after a bit of persuading she then agreed and set up what was to become the 1st Buckingham Palace Brownie and Guide packs, over which she was to become the Captain. At the time Princess Margaret was only six years old and therefore too young to join, however Princess Elizabeth persuaded

Violet, known by this time as 'Captain', to include Princess Margaret lifting Margaret's skirt and saying "You can't say those aren't a very fine pair of hiking legs, Miss Synge."[4] It was decided that Princess Margaret could be made a Brownie so that she could join in with the Palace Girl Guides.

The main dilemma that faced Violet in setting up a Girl Guide company for the heir to the throne was that in all her previous fifteen years of Guiding, her policy had been to inspire the children in her care to let themselves go and run around and enjoy the

Christabel, Robert, Violet, children unknown boy, Pamela.

outside adventures and dangers of childhood, encouraging children to use their wits, be daring and ready for any emergency. Not quite what the royal household would have necessarily had in mind for the royal Princesses. In her book *Royal Guides*, Violet recalled that before she had met Princess Elizabeth she imagined that with a life of such privilege, she "could not remain unspoilt," but had been reassured by the royal nanny, 'Crawfie' over the phone, " You will find them just like any ordinary little girls",[5] Straight away Violet was won over by the Princess's charm and naturalness.

My mother was one of 14 Guides and Brownies recruited by her aunt to the newly formed 1st Buckingham Palace Girl Guide group. All the girls were told they must live up to the Girl Guide motto, 'Be Prepared', patrols were formed and thus began a small group of Guides both encouraged to have as much fun as possible, learn valuable outdoors skills and learn about citizenship and loyalty. It was decided that Buckingham Palace Summer

Princess Elizabeth front right, marching with gas masks.
Princess Margaret left 4 back. Pamela 3rd from right.

Left: Violet Synge, Princess Margaret.

House was to be the weekly meeting place. The children who had been invited to join the Buckingham Palace Guides were nervous and shy in the company of the Royal Household and my mother's aunt, Violet, also had her own shyness to contend with. She decided that 'wild escapades' were needed to break the ice and very quickly had the children running round the Palace gardens playing games. My mother was a child who simply had no concept of shyness and was quite fearless, so she was quickly utilised by her aunt when the Guides were overwhelmed by the royal household, or to chivvy the Royal Princesses when needed.

My mother's favourite Guiding story, which she told my sisters and me when we were children, was of an occasion when she, Princess Elizabeth and several others hid on top of a haystack in Windsor Great Park. Royal courtiers were worried because they had seemingly lost the heir to the throne and a search party was organised. The girls were discovered by King George VI who had crawled on hands and knees into the hay to find them. Violet was so angry with the girls that she took away the ladder as punishment and told them that they would have to find their own way down. She wrote "I contented myself with taking the ladder away in revenge and left them to get down as best they could."[6]

On one occasion at the Palace a message was given to Violet, seemingly from Scotland Yard, to warn her that two lunatics were somewhere in the Palace grounds. She immediately dispatched the Guides to go and catch them. The lunatics were caught, overpowered and pinned down, only to find that one of them was the royal nanny 'Crawfie' and the other a Guide Lieutenant. Between 1940 and 1942 the group was disbanded due to the war but it started up again in 1942. During the winter it was decided that the Guides would meet in the Waterloo Chamber in Windsor Castle but if the weather was even half decent they would all go out to the Castle garden. Hikes were organised in Windsor Great Park, food was cooked on camp fires and challenges and escapades were organized. At the end of the day they would all be driven back to London on the royal bus. In 1941 my mother had turned 18 and had meanwhile joined the Postal and Telegraph Censorship Department in Brook Street, Holborn where she was trained to

Camping at Frogmore, Windsor Great Park
Princess Elizabeth front, Pamela second right.

work as a temporary woman clerk. It must have been an odd feeling to go back to the Girl Guides and climb haystacks after having joined the adult world which was now at war.

In 1942 Violet, aware of the sadness of their changing world, wrote, "The loveliness of our surroundings, the response of the children and their absorption in the various activities of Guiding were a brief respite from the anguish of those times and a glimpse into a world that might have been."[7]

In 1944 the war was at its worst and Windsor was badly affected by the bombing, nicknamed 'Flying bomb alley'.[8] Despite this the Royal Guides continued their weekly meetings in the Windsor Castle grounds. They were told that they had five seconds to dive for cover if the engine of the planes above them cut out. On one occasion they were hiking in the Castle grounds when a 'doodlebug' came down in the vicinity. Violet told them all to lie flat and, noticing that Princess Margaret was standing close to her, contemplated hurling herself on top of the young princess but did not know which would be of more danger to the princess, the doodlebug's descent or being squashed by herself. She decided against hurling herself on top of the young princess. The doodlebug then hit a nearby house, killing its owner.

On several occasions the company was joined by the King and Queen, so when my mother sang the National Anthem as Guides all around the country do, she sang it with real passion. Even decades later when she, my sisters and I would watch the annual televised Queen's Christmas Day speech, she would make us stand during the playing of the National Anthem. Our protests of "but Mummy the Queen can't see us", were totally ignored.

My mother's biggest lifelong pleasure, discovered during her time as a Guide, was the joy of singing with others. They would sit round log fires under the Castle walls singing songs in English and French, Negro spirituals and madrigals, and she could sing in several parts. This gave her a passion for singing which would later see her singing in Middle Eastern cathedrals, war torn London, Bermuda, Buckingham Palace and Windsor Castle with the royal family. It was also the beginning of a lifetime friendship with the Princesses and the royal household where she was, years later, still singing with the Princesses in a weekly Madrigal Society which was sometimes joined by boys from Eton and occasionally by the Eton Choir. The rehearsals were usually held in Buckingham Palace or Windsor Castle. The notice of choir rehearsals would arrive in the form of telegrams from the Lady in Waiting, informing her of the time and place of the rehearsal and were concluded with and their "Royal Highnesses hope so very much that Miss Synge will be able to come again".

My mother relished the fun and adventure of the 1st Buckingham Palace Guides under her aunt Violet's captaincy, taking on the duties, tests and challenges of Guiding with enthusiasm and threw herself into the fun and games in the Palace Gardens in a time of short lived innocence. In her early days of Guiding she spent time charging around the Palace, carefree and full of optimism, not knowing that the world of her childhood was about to be torn apart by war on an unprecedented scale. The values that had been instilled in her were those of an age when Britain still had an Empire and the most powerful Navy in the world. She and her peers took it for granted that England was one of the most powerful countries in the world, a country over which her friend Princess Elizabeth was shortly to become sovereign.

The precious time that my mother spent in the royal household on the eve of World War II was to inform her decision to take an active role during the war and afterwards the Cold War whatever the danger. The training and ethos of the Guides Company along with the dignity and sense of duty that was displayed by the King, Queen, the royal Princesses and her aunt in the role of 'Guide Captain', gave her a strong sense of duty to King and Country. This combined with the active way her parents were involved with World War I set her on a determined path to do her bit. When, on September 1st 1939 war was declared, my mother was 17 years old and was more than ready and willing to get involved in defending her country.

Many years later, when we were children, she would train my sisters and me to walk with books on our heads for deportment; she also taught us to curtsy to the Queen in preparation for when we would meet her; she, of course, played the role of the Queen. My sisters and I generally thought that it would never happen, and even if it did it seemed ridiculously old fashioned and annoying. Then one day, when we were teenagers, we were all taken out of school for the day and told to wear our best dresses. In the car my mother told us we were going to have drinks with the Queen; we were staggered. We turned up at a friend's house, walked in and there in the centre of their drawing-room was the Queen standing alone in a bright red dress and wearing a chunky stone bracelet around her wrist. She said "hello Pam", and they picked up from there. The Queen was relaxed in the privacy of this house but it was clear she did not suffer fools.

Princess Elizabeth 1944.

CHAPTER 3
Evacuation to America

By 1940 Britain was being extensively bombed by German planes and cities were their main targets. On the 7th September 1940 the German air force began to concentrate on bombing London and, nearly 2,000 people were killed or wounded in the first night of the bombing, Other British cities were bombed night after night for months and by the end of the Blitz, as it became known, two million houses had been destroyed, 32,000 civilians killed and a further 87,000 were seriously injured. [9]

Four million British children were evacuated; most were sent to live with families who lived in the countryside where it was considered safer from the bombing than in the cities; some children were sent abroad but most were sent to homes around Britain. If these children had not been evacuated the list of those killed and seriously injured would have been much longer.

Over the summer of 1940, my grandparents, Robert and Christabel, made the incredibly painful decision, as did millions of other parents at various times throughout the bombings, to evacuate their children. It was decided that they would send them to America. Robert's mother was American and there were aunts and cousins to call on for help. It was also decided that my mother, who was 17 years old at the time, was old enough to escort her younger siblings, Allen and Gillian, to the safety of a country not at war. America had not yet joined the war and did not do so until

December 1941 after the Japanese bombed Pearl Harbour. My mother was not happy about the plan and felt that she should stay and help with the war effort but resigned herself to the responsibility of escorting her younger siblings to America and so agreed.

Between July and September 1940 the British Prime Minister Winston Churchill set up the Children's Overseas Reception Board, which organised the evacuation of an estimated 2,664 British children to countries like Canada, Australia, America and New Zealand.

On September 18th 1940 the passenger ship SS *City of Benares* was taking 90 British evacuated children and voluntary escorts like nurses and doctors from Britain to Canada. The ship was torpedoed by a German submarine. 77 of the evacuated children lost their lives along with many others. In response Winston Churchill cancelled the plan to relocate British children abroad. The evacuated children trying to cross the Atlantic were among Britain's first civilian casualties of the war. In this context it may not have been an easy decision for my grandparents, Robert and Christabel, to expose their children to the danger of being torpedoed. One can only surmise that they thought it less of a danger than keeping them in England.

On the 5th July 1940 my mother, Allen and Gillian departed by boat from Holyhead aboard the SS *Washington*, a luxury liner owned by the United States. When the boat reached its destination, New York, there was a swarm of journalists waiting to photograph the evacuated English children, eager to capture the look of awe on their faces as they disembarked onto American soil for the first time.

My mother's brother Allen wrote a fictional account of his evacuation to America, and this was included in the book *The Evacuees*[10] where he wrote about the large ship that was to take him away from his homeland, which he described as "an impression of towering metal and huge sailors in small white hats, an unforgettable smell compounded of diesel oil, peanut butter and seawater". In this account he described a young boy's first glimpse of New York with its 'Dinky Toy' taxis and described the meeting of colourful aunts who couldn't wait to show him and his fictional brother the sights of New York. Allen wrote in this account about the shock of a young boy seeing New York for the first time as a city that was not blacked out at night and not at war, as London was at the time, and vibrant with what he described as "dizzy neon messages, those flashing beer bottles and glowing Colas." He wrote that these things "seemed only to illuminate a brutal peace".[11]

He also described with great sadness the point when he was told that he would be separated from his fictional brother, who was then taken off to live with a different relative. In real life he and his siblings were separated. Allen wrote about the emotions of his fictional self, on the day of the separation: "I lay on the sofa in Aunt Dorothy's apartment and wept for everything I had known."[12] America's peace and London's war at that time could not have been more different, and seen through the eyes of a young boy all the more poignant.

Allen then went on to describe in his fictional account that their parents had sent them with an important message that he and his brother must tell the Americans that it was imperative for America to join the war and to explain to them for what we were fighting. In real life his parents had told their children that they must do their best to convince their American cousins to join the war. Allen later described in *The Talking Book*[13] a train journey to Maine from New York with my mother who was taking him to stay with family in 1940. My mother was not impressed by America's refusal to join the war. It so happened that Rear Admiral Byrd was on the train. Byrd was a highly decorated naval officer for his efforts during World War I. On realising who he was, my mother approached him and gave him a telling off for not joining in the War. He, according to Allen, seemed to listen attentively and they got to Maine without incident.

There were also benefits for Allen living in America which perhaps may have only been seen with hindsight after the pain of separation from his parents and his homeland had died down. He was an asthmatic child and suffered terribly from repeated asthma attacks. During the New York winter of 1940 it was decided that my mother was to take him to stay with their great aunt, Eufrasia Tucker, who lived in Tucson, a city in Arizona's Sonoran Desert, surrounded by multiple mountain ranges. There the air was hot and dry and the family thought it would be better for his health. For the remainder of his life Allen said that his health was never so good as when he was in Arizona; his asthma all but disappeared during the time that he was there.

Allen centre, Pamela right.

Another benefit for the three siblings was the opportunity that evacuation gave them to get to know and love their extended American family. Allen became fond of another aunt, Anne. In *The Evacuees*, edited by B.S Johnson, Johnson writes, "Allen Synge achieved a rapport with a touching, brittle, fragile aunt in New York. He gives me the notion that evacuation to America, comfort apart, may have had special psychological compensations."[14] Getting to know his American family would not have been so straightforward if it were not for his evacuation with his siblings and that legacy of love and support has been passed down to the next generation of cousins across the pond.

For my mother, her time in America was, to some extent, a time of frustration and rebellion but also a time of adventure and opportunity. It was also a time when she learned to express her feelings by writing poems. This she continued to do all through her life, using poetry as an outlet for her emotions. In a poem that she wrote about her experience called *The Refugee*, Pamela wrote:

> *A deep and aching sorrow*
> *Tears at my heart,*
> *But I must block my ears,*
> *For I cannot do my part;*
> *I'd die for my country,*
> *But this can never be,*
> *I must love, and laugh, and live*
> *A worthless refugee.*[15]

My mother found the journey away from her homeland slow and tortuous, describing in her poetry her wish to jump off the boat and risk drowning in order to try and swim back home. Despite her sadness, the time that she shared with her brother Allen in Arizona was a time that she cherished. It was filled with horse riding through the Sonoran Desert, surrounded by six foot cactus plants, where she described in a letter to her parents, "the horses being amazingly surefooted and intelligent they did not bump into cactuses or cause landslides".

During her time in Arizona she took up oil painting and joined the local theatre group to act in a production of Aristophanes' comedy *Lysistrata*.

My mother and Allen also visited a town called Tombstone, which was known for its Wild West history, where resident ghosts were said to haunt the town theatre called the Bird Cage and where outlaws were buried among the townsfolk in the local cemetery. The experience made an impression on her and she wrote about her experience in a poem called *Tombstone* "'The graves on the hill are heaped with stones, Carelessly thrown over murderers' bones."

Pamela in Arizona.

My mother was initially sent to live in New York with her aunt, Anne Tucker, where it was decided that she would 'come out' in American society and do the debutante season. Gloria Vanderbilt, who was an heiress and socialite, was a debutante at the time. My mother was made a member of the Bar Harbor Club, where socialites and celebrities gathered and enjoyed meeting other high society guests, such as the Fords and Rockefellers.

Despite the opportunities that had come her way, my mother was furious that, as she saw it, at a time when her homeland was at war and her parents were doing their part, she should be stuck as a refugee far away from her homeland and the war effort; it did not seem like the time or the place for such frivolity as debutante balls and sitting around in clubs. She resolved to help the war effort and asked her father to find a job for her.

Before leaving America, however, she met an Ottoman prince of New York high society, Prince Fahreddin of Turkey, in the Bar Harbor Club where he frequently hosted parties. The prince had been exiled in 1924 and never returned to Turkey. He was struck by my mother's beauty and asked her to sit for a photo shoot for *American Vogue*. She agreed and returned home with some very striking photographs of her dressed up in feather boas and beautiful dresses.

Photograph of Pamela taken for American Vogue
by Prince Fahreddin of Turkey.

Pamela learning to parachute USA.

During my mother's time in America she exchanged correspondence with her cousin, Charles Liddell, who was in the Rifle Brigade which was stationed in the Egyptian desert. She wrote of her frustrations of life in

America to which Charles responded, "The Americans are the people who must take the lead when this war is over to bring about some sort of federation of all English speaking peoples gradually forming into an empire of dominions that will be so strong that nothing dare challenge it or be outside the league".

The youngest of the three siblings, Gillian, said in later life that the experience of being evacuated and separated from her parents at the age of six was so distressing that she had totally erased it from her memory.

Gillian was sent to stay with an aunt and uncle in Chestnut Hill and lived with them for four years. During the summers she would meet up with her brother, Allen, in Castine, a beautiful coastal town in Maine. One of Allen's friends was a young Marine called George Ames, a Bostonian. A romance developed between Gillian and George during those summers that was to last a lifetime. In 1950 Gillian returned to Castine to visit George and in 1952 they got married. She remained in America for the rest of her life bringing up a family of four children and then enjoying ten grandchildren. One pleasure she did not give up her entire life was doing the *Telegraph* Crossword Puzzle every day. She threw herself into American life; the only thing she yearned for was the English spring.

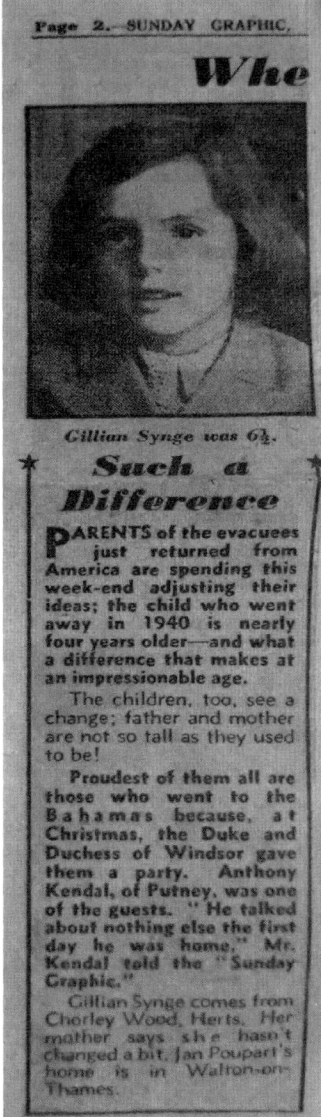

Page 2.—SUNDAY GRAPHIC.

Whe

Gillian Synge was 6½.

Such a Difference

PARENTS of the evacuees just returned from America are spending this week-end adjusting their ideas; the child who went away in 1940 is nearly four years older—and what a difference that makes at an impressionable age.

The children, too, see a change; father and mother are not so tall as they used to be!

Proudest of them all are those who went to the Bahamas because, at Christmas, the Duke and Duchess of Windsor gave them a party. Anthony Kendal, of Putney, was one of the guests. " He talked about nothing else the first day he was home," Mr. Kendal told the "Sunday Graphic."

Gillian Synge comes from Chorley Wood, Herts. Her mother says she hasn't changed a bit. Jan Poupart's home is in Walton-on-Thames.

Evacuee Gillian Synge.

CHAPTER 4
Secrets: British Censorship in Bermuda

On 29th September 1941, when she was eighteen years old, my mother's prayer was answered and she was sent to Bermuda. Her profession on her passport was 'Government Official.' With the help of her father in the Foreign Office, it was decided that she should join the Postal and Telegraph Censorship Department. Before departing, she swore an oath under the Official Secrets Act: unauthorised disclosure of information under the Act would lead to imprisonment. For the whole of her life, she was afraid and did not dare speak of her work.

The Postal and Telegraph Censorship Department, which had been taken over by the War Office, was initially censorship based in London but, because of London being a target for bombing, it was moved first to Liverpool, where it was thought there would not be extensive bombing but that did not prove to be the case, and then to Bermuda, where it was housed in the Hamilton Princess Hotel, Pembroke. There it remained for the duration of the war, with top secret work being carried out in its 13 rooms. After the war it was disbanded.

Officially my mother was trained as a temporary secretary. Bermuda essentially provided a filter through which all correspondence in the western hemisphere was inspected. It was also an important British naval base and a United Kingdom sovereign state, safe from air raids.

1500 British intelligence officers, academics and code-breakers went to Bermuda. Teams of young, usually attractive, English women made up mainly of university students and linguists became known as 'censorettes'. Their job was to sift through mail intercepted between Europe and the United States, but mainly going from America to Germany, for information that might be of use to the enemy and to work out who was collaborating with the enemy. There was an idea that women with good legs made good codebreakers, not a theory that would work in our feminist world today. The 'censorettes' looked for evidence of enemy agents' operations in America before it entered the war. They also tried to prevent money and jewellery from getting to the enemy. Letters were steamed open with small kettles to look for evidence and then put together again to look as though they had not been tampered with and returned. They could return the mail with no trace of tampering although they would sometimes replace a letter with a forged replica. Bermuda developed the top scientific testing laboratory out of all British censorship departments where letters were tested for secret inks. All correspondence sent to or from Europe was intercepted, examined and photographed. Addresses were put on blacklists if they were deemed suspicious. The Department was used as a training ground with censors learning the ropes before being moved to other stations.

My mother was one of many who worked in Bermuda at the time. Around 200,000 letters a day would pass through the Department to be scrutinised by the censors looking for hidden microdots and secret ink messages, all of which had to be done without the items looking like they had been opened. The team managed to read secret coded letters from what turned out to be the largest Nazi espionage operation in America based in New York, which was sending reports of allied ships in New York harbour and other sensitive information to Nazis in Europe. The Nazis would then send submarines to the Atlantic to have the British ships torpedoed, and many lost their lives as a result. The leader of the ring was a German who went under the name of Joe K who ran a sophisticated spy ring. His real name was Kurt Frederick Ludwig. He sent letters that had secret code written in invisible ink that only one chemical could reveal.

One of the censors acquired the chemical and the real text was revealed. The code breaker who made the discovery was an examiner called Nadya Gardner, who secretly went through the mail that came in diplomatic pouches. Ludwig was arrested by MI5's deputy director Guy Liddell and sent to gaol, but avoided being executed for treason because America had not yet joined the war.

Bermuda had the reputation both for its pink sandy beaches and as an island of pirates and thieves so when the British arrived and began to seize mail, contraband and jewellery from ships and boats passing through, they were following an established tradition. Mail examiners scrutinised thousands of letters a day to ensure they didn't contain information which could be potentially damaging to the British war effort. [16]

When America officially joined the war, in December 1941, it worked with the British censors in Bermuda under the wing of a Canadian, William Stephenson, code name 'Intrepid', to prevent Nazi spies and saboteurs working in North America. In order to support the censorship operation, America sent as many ships and planes via Bermuda as possible. By April 1944, America had built and set up a navy base in Bermuda so there were increasing numbers of both British and Americans on the small island. The U.S. Army Air Force operated the air traffic section of the base. The Bermuda base became a vital link in air and sea traffic between the United States and Europe both during and after the war as a 'stop off place.' Troops were able to rest, recover and receive medical treatment, while military personnel used the facilities to hold conferences. [17]

When there were many ships in the harbour my mother, who was working in the basement of the hotel, had to work at speed for many hours in a row. She found the hours long in the humid heat. Sometimes art works were confiscated by the censors. On August 8th 1940, a shipment of some 500 "Old Masters" was discovered on the SS *Excalibur* of the American Export Line which had docked in Bermuda at the Princess Hotel. Amongst them were priceless artworks by Renoir, Cezanne, Manet and Picasso. These significant art works had been confiscated by the Gestapo and other German authorities from Jewish individuals and families. [18]

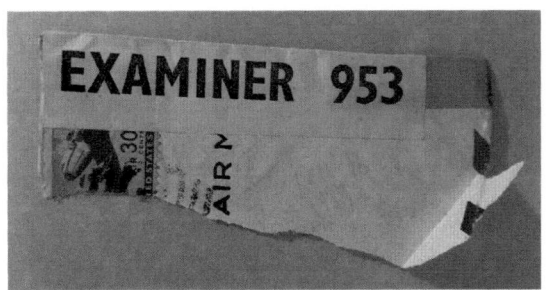

My mother was examiner 953.

Once America joined the war after Pearl Harbour they took over the Bermuda censorship department and most of the British left.

My mother worked and trained in Bermuda for six months during which she was sent to live in the Hotel Bermudiana which had also been taken over by the British and used for residential quarters. She described cascades of crimson flowers and scents to make a man swoon. In one of her poems she wrote:

> *Rumbling, racing down sickly lanes*
> *A wooden cart that is long and low,*
> *With flickering candle-lamp's orange glow,*
> *And a man standing holding the reins.*
> *His whip is flourished, and fast they go*
> *Through distance into the silence – so*
> *Spell is broke and safe are the lanes.*

She wrote fairly disparagingly about hotel life and described Bermuda as oppressive. The island was small and isolated. From July to September it was both hot and humid. There was no entertainment so the British had to create their own. The censorship department set up amateur dramatic societies, a choir, theatrical and singing groups and the workers could swim in the hotel pool or play tennis. All pursuits were a comfort between long days and nights of relentless work. Food was plentiful unlike the rationed lives of people at home.

In January 1942, whilst my mother was in Bermuda, the Prime Minister Winston Churchill paid a twenty-four hour surprise visit to the island.

In an address to the House of Assembly he thanked the Bermudians and the British for their efforts.

Whilst my mother was steaming open mail in the basement of the Bermudiana, unbeknown to her, the future love of her life, who was later to be my father, Charles Fane, was sailing past on one of the convoys sent to Russia carrying essential supplies for the Soviets. He was in the Merchant Navy. Enemy submarines were in the Atlantic and the danger of being hit by the enemy was enormous and many of the convoys were destroyed.

My mother left Bermuda on 29th April 1942 and setting sail for Liverpool where she arrived twelve days later.

London

My mother returned to live in the family home in Chorleywood. In July 1942 she started to work again in the London Postal and Telegraph Cipher Department where she trained to become an Examiner Grade 2.

From 1st October 1941 until 28th April 1942 she worked as a temporary woman clerk in Bermuda and then from July 1942 to September 1945 as an Examiner Grade 2. In 1945 all work there was terminated due to the end of the war. The temporary secretaries were generally not career civil servants but were doing their job as their war work, some of whom like my mother were connected to the diplomatic service. My mother also worked during this time in Leconfield House in Curzon Street where MI5 moved their headquarters in 1945. During her time there she told her mother and siblings that they were not allowed to walk down the street with her as she was concerned for her anonymity and their safety; she had the idea that Germans with syringes were around and could hurt them.

In her 1942/43 diaries, she mentioned a life of parties, of singing in Buckingham Palace interspersed with grim commuting to Chorleywood and tough and relentless work. She was single.

In 1943 the royal household put on a production of Aladdin. It is unclear if my mother was a guest or an unimportant actor. My grandparents were invited to the performance and given a very strict dress code.

CHAPTER 5
Egypt: 'A' Force Technical Unit

I n 1944 Egypt held a strategic position for the British: it was a gateway to Iran and Iraq which provided valuable oil essential for planes, tanks and ships. Its location was a hub between Africa, Asia and Europe. Control of Egypt meant good communication lines and vital air and sea routes. The Suez Canal was used as a route to move troops and material between Europe and the Pacific. The British occupation of Egypt, however, was not popular. Artemis Cooper wrote in her book, *Cairo in the War: 1939-1945* "if Egypt had realised how weak Britain was during the constant bombardment by German bombers it may not have wished to provide labour and facilities on which the British war machine in the Middle East was to depend."[19]

"In the autumn of 1940 the half million strong population of Cairo had been increased by only a few thousand British and Empire troops; by the following spring, these numbered 35,000."[20]

In war torn Britain there was rationing and by contrast in Cairo there was all the food that was not available at home and the streets smelled of fresh coffee and local fruit and vegetables. Even butter was available in abundance. Having served in Bermuda, my mother would have already experienced the contrast of leaving a cold Britain, bombarded from the air and tormented by rationing and lack of food, for a warmer climate with no bombs or rations, but her time both in Bermuda and then in Cairo had different challenges and dangers.

On 14th January 1944 the British Postal and Telegraph Censorship Department under the command of the War Office sent her to Egypt after having trained her to work in censorship as an Examiner Grade 2 in London. She sailed by boat from Liverpool, arriving in Alexandria 17 days later on 30th January, where she joined a team of censors working in the censorship laboratory of the Montcrieff House Cairo 'A' Force Technical Unit.

'A' Force was the name of a deception department founded in March 1940 by the British Military Intelligence Officer, Dudley Clarke. He was its head until the end of the war, during which time he created fake invasion plans to keep the Axis from spotting the real ones, and became a master of strategic military deception tactics. Clarke created an army which did not really exist to confuse the enemy. He called it the "First Special Air Service". Everything about it was fake, but it quickly became a real unit and is now known as the SAS, famous for being the most highly trained special force in the world.

In 'A' Force my mother worked in a team under Major Titterington, who was a forger producing all the department's fake passports and other documents. He had the reputation of being the world's greatest forger. He was also tasked with opening the diplomatic bags of neutral nations so that Clarke could read their contents before sealing them back up again.[21] My mother worked using the skills of opening diplomatic bags and mail that she had acquired whilst working in Bermuda, and like her work in Bermuda, it often involved long night shifts in order to open and reseal the diplomatic bags as and when they came in.

'A' Force Technical Unit was responsible for anti German Espionage Censorship in the German Centre of Espionage. The Egyptians were not at war with Germany at this time and Egypt was occupied by the British. My mother also worked for Tommi Fairclough, a friend and colleague of my grandfather Robert. Tommi used to escort the female officers home through Cairo in taxis through the night to keep them safe.

One of the 'A' Force operations of deception was described by the British Judge and Naval Intelligence Officer, the Hon. Ewen E.S Montagu QC, in a note, "We successfully put over much deception about, for instance, radar, mines, torpedoes, submarine detection (thus helping to protect our use of ULTRA deciphered signals to sink U-boats and protect convoys)."[22] My father Charles Fane was on one of the convoys that 'A' Force helped to protect whilst my mother was working there but they were yet to meet.

Paula Ormerod described the atmosphere in Cairo at the time in her book, *Cairo Child*, "Cairo was by now, allegedly, swarming with spies and secret agents. Most German and Italians had been interned, but mysteriously there still remained a great many enemy civilians at large and letters and cables had to be rigorously examined."[23]

Work and Rest

Much of the censorship work in Cairo that my mother was involved with meant long day and night shifts often for days in a row with potential health hazards round every corner. She wrote to her parents, "I have become known for health and strength which is amusing when one considers the pale and skinny child I was. I have passed all records. People who have avoided dysentery and jaundice all get 'gyppy tummy' little fevers and horrible bites headaches and pains. I have had one cold, you must not mind my boasting." Certainly, one theme that went through her letters to her family was that she had a strong constitution and a strong personality, seeming to thrive and come into her own at times when several of her colleagues were struggling with illness or loss of nerve due to exhaustion.

The climate also had its challenges for the English who were used to much gentler seasons. My mother wrote to her family in December 1944, "My room is cold. All these cool white arches were built to repel all sun and warmth: which is ideal in summer, but cold now in a stark bare penetrating way. Ghostly winds from miles of distant desert seem to condense in them. Fires make no impression upon marble halls: this cold would seep into the great pyramid. It is not as cold as England. It does not make you shiver, it is quiet and deadly and clammy and would shrewdly find the way into anything that man invented to keep it out. However the days are glorious. The sun is loving and the air like champagne." In January 1945 she wrote, "A cold khamshea blowing. I think I dislike it more than a hot one. All the dust and rubbish of Cairo blows round and round in silly little eddies (I have just washed my hair, bad luck!) The trees shiver, the sky is dimmed and the air pink, but I take its intense howl. Like the Sirocco it has a taunting effect on the nerves. 'Dishcloth' and someone else in the office felt they must have a fight with someone. Some felt gloomy, others slightly like murder. Murder actually is overlooked in the real desert khan sheen."

My mother's first cousin Charles Liddell was in the Rifle Brigade based in the Egyptian desert during the war and he and my mother wrote many letters to each other. In one of his letters to her from the desert he wrote "Life out here is much the same, it is much colder in fact very cold and there are no flies, but instead it blows steadily and blows the dust into one's eyes ears mouth nose and food, and of course we don't get much water to wash it off so we are pretty filthy some of us even have confessed to fleas, but luckily I have so far escaped their attention."

In October 1944, the woman in charge of the Department that my mother was working for in 'A' Force Unit suffered a breakdown. In a letter to her parents dated 15th October 44 my mother wrote,

"The woman in charge is losing her nerve and has violent panic attacks and hysteria practically every hour and it falls to my lot to undo her damage and prevent her from going quite gaga". The woman in question had not long before been mentioned in dispatches. My mother described how the other 15 ladies in the department came to her weeping and saying their "nerves can't stand it a moment longer." The lady was hastily removed and my mother was left in charge of 15 significantly older colleagues with the job of calming them down despite having to work punishing night shifts that ended at 6am.

Relishing the challenge, she wrote: "But I must admit that I rather enjoy coping with it all and them all. I have had a little talk with them all and I think overturned revolution, luckily 'the boys' realised that she was quite impossible and making everyone lose their nerve, so there was a sudden arrangement for her to be flown elsewhere for a bit and I was to be put in full charge of the fifteen shaken remnants! This was over the heads of several more antique members which I thought might cause a new outbreak of hostilities. However they were all very nice and helpful – only a few remarks passed as to how it was easy for me as I had no nerves at all, to which I replied that it was only a matter of control. I said it was absolutely essential to this work and that they must all hang on for a few days before she went. It would have been easier to do most of the work and all of the organising un-aided by her! But unfortunately the scene fell through and the sighs of relief could not be heaved. She returned just when everything was getting efficient and calm and so I was back at scratch. But she is going soon and 'the boys' have told her she must do much less work. If I am to do more work it is worth it having less fuss and panic. I feel very sorry for her and have I think forwarded several soothing and sensible ploys for her. I have inspired her with ideas of everyone being brought up to a good standard by her supervision and encouragement, told her who is nervy and who might be good at what (this of course with a weather eye to my own escape, for as you can probably see they really cannot do without me, which could sound smug if it were not so very depressing). However I am going to write to the 'Old Man' telling him to make a definite bid for the early spring and shall tell all in plenty of time.

Poor old thing – she has been very kind to me and will at the moment only listen to me. She was always a little hectic but never like this. I hope she'll pull herself together. Not so very long ago she got a 'mention in dispatches' one of 'the boys' is no longer scared by her but is by her effect on others the other never was. They have both been most helpful and sensible. They know that I have been working terribly hard and will see that I have a rest when things straighten out. Myrtle Winter is a help too and very nice. I'm sure when Sheila is back and Edy away we will have time to get through several reforms and restore the others to self-confidence without being bossy or officious. I think they are all ready to help for they are a nice lot really – but one never knows. I think they mostly like and respect as, in spite of this, usual slight and perhaps just prejudice against youth in authority."

On July 26th 1945 the Director General of the Postal and Telegraph Censorship department in London wrote to the Anglo Egyptian Censorship testing section in Cairo.

"Director General's letter of 15th June and my letter of the 4th July referring to provision of an A.C Special Sorter.

It became clear beyond all matter of doubt to Stebbing, Acting Deputy Controller, Anglo-Egyptian Censorship that Mrs Murray was temperamentally unfitted to continue in the post of D.A.C Testing section.

Seeking my approval he informed Mrs. Murray of the reasons for considering a change imperative and immediate. Mrs Murray has as a result tendered her resignation on 24th July. The actual date on which she will cease to draw pay is under consideration.

Stebbing deplored the necessity for seeking approval to take this step in view of the admirable work Mrs Murray has carried out over a long period. It is essential that the Testing Section shall continue to work to full capacity, and to obtain maximum efficiency it is essential there shall be harmony (particularly where there is 100% female staff). I am fully satisfied that harmony in the conditions pertaining was unobtainable.

Stebbing feels reasonably satisfied that there are two ladies in the Section who are qualified and fitted respectively to assume charge of the Section and 'Cover' in the case of absence. He proposes to give both a trial, and should they prove entirely satisfactory he will seek approval to appoint one of them to the vacancy caused by Mrs Murray's resignation."[24] It might be reasonable to conclude that the boss in my mother's letter was Mrs Murray.

One of my mother's colleagues in 'A' Force was Myrtle Winter, Liaison Officer, Head, Communications Department, British Foreign Service, Egypt and London 1944-1950 Assistant Censor, Special Branch, British Imperial Censorship, Bermuda 1940-1950. She spoke English, French, German, Italian and Arabic. Not surprising that my mother wrote to her parents that 'most of our talent is here in the Middle East.' Perhaps worth noting that the outstanding women doing their part got little or no mention compared to their male counterparts.

My mother's friend, Sheila Jaimeson, had parents living in Cairo, during the time that my mother and she were working there. Her parents were Methodists and she would sometimes ask my mother to lunch with her parents. The lunches tended to be bleak, the father was austere and

Some members of the 'A' Force office top left to right
Muriel, Honour, Myrtle, bottom left to right Sheila,
Edy, Titters, Prince M Emin Haidar, Unknown.

frightening so that even my mother remained silent throughout. The meals were bland and the portions small.

In January 1945, after many gruelling months of relentless work Sheila and my mother were granted time off. In a letter to her parents my mother wrote, "A day off in the sun after having worked most of Saturday, Sunday and Monday. Further than that, the office, in a burst of magnanimity allowed Sheila and I to go off for a week's leave together, so on Wednesday 7th all being well, we shall set off for Aswan in upper Egypt."

From Aswan she wrote a letter to her parents,

Cataract Hotel Aswan Egypt February 9th 1945

My dearest family,
Aswan is a charming place. One arrives at the sunny station in a very friendly bustle after which one finds oneself firmly established in the most enchanting bus you have ever seen. It belongs to the hotel and is bright yellow with a frill round the top of the hood, something like a pram, a brass switch for a starter and an enormous brass motor horn. It has, needless to say, enormous difficulty getting

up the last steep hill and one is suspended, braked, in the middle of the steep hill wondering whether one should get out and push, or whether the slightest movement would send it spinning down the hill again. Eventually one puffs over the top and through the gates into a courtyard which makes one gasp and laugh because quite suddenly it is a land of musical comedy or a scene from the Barber of Seville, a very bright, unreal circular building with balconies, curtains and striped awnings, and stiff beds of very bright flowers. Very bright and nonsensical and so different from the arched and carpeted oriental interior.

I must say that the first day we were so full of accumulated tiredness that we could do little else but sleep and the beds are so huge and the linen so very soft. The servants are good and the whole place most luxurious. We have but one criticism. We found animals in the soup. I summoned the head waiter and the under head waiter, they both tried to say "it is of the soup," I said it was in the soup and had six legs and would not, I hoped, appear again. Since then there has been great civility all round and no more animals.

After a week of sailing, riding, shopping, sunbathing and exploring the two friends returned back to Cairo suntanned, rested and cheerful.

Sheila and Pamela at Aswan.

When my mother had some time off, she would go to the Gezira Sporting Club situated in Zamalek. It was in an area preferred by the British because it was by the river Nile and slightly cooler than further into the city of Cairo.

The land had been formally leased to the British military in the 18th century and was initially only for the use of British military officers but during the war it allowed society's elite and European aristocrats to become members. My mother wrote to her parents, "I so often wish you could be here to walk round the race course with me, or sit in long chairs by the playing field and order nice things on trays. The famous Gezira

Club is delightful and we are more than lucky to be war time members, so cheaply. In the old days you did not become a member until you were too old to be able to do anything with it, or dead."

Pamela at the Gezira Sporting Club.

The Club was frequented by some of the more colourful of the foreign guests. Cairo at this time was a city buzzing with so many different nationalities, some of whom were European aristocrats in exile, as was amusingly reflected on by my mother's brother Allen who wrote in a letter to her:

"After turning countless little Brit officers down I have come to the conclusion that you will fall in love with one of the following:
1 Yugoslav Bolshi Partisan
2 Member of Bulgarian Armistice Commission

3 Fighting Greek
4 Arab"

My mother's response was:

"This covers most of the Middle East and gives me a large field of choice. Tom laughed a great deal over the letter and is inclined to think that Allen must expect a Yugoslav Bolshi Partisan for a brother-in-law. There are several alarming looking Yugoslavs at Gezira Sporting Club, Soskonoskovitch who always wears a towel around his neck and dark slanting glasses and walks like an aged leopard, Blooditch who swings his arms like a gorilla, humming always a little signature tune through loose teeth, and often throwing girls into the "Zuimming Bool" and a rather plebeian looking Count with flopping hands and flapping feet."

In a letter written at the Gezira Sporting Club, Tuesday 29th January 1945 she wrote:

"My dearest Mummy and Daddy,
I had a day off today. Having worked three exceedingly long days at the office, and spent it most pleasantly in a long chair at the club at the edge of the cricket pitch, listening to the 'clack' of balls from all the surrounding games. Which vary from American Grid Football and hockey to bowls and croquet. Having lately given the government so much of my time I consider myself entitled to use their rather pleasant little sheets of white note paper. I am afraid I have missed out a week which was unavoidable as I have been working very hard indeed.
I feel very well though and they all say I look well. The weekends are something like this – all day Friday and until six am on Saturday morning, in again at nine o'clock on Saturday and work until lunchtime Sunday morning and twelve hours on Monday."

On their days off some of the office members would take boat trips on the river Nile.

A houseboat party, Pamela front row 4 from left.

During my mother's time in Cairo, there were dances and parties often held at Montcrieff House. In a letter to her parents, my mother wrote, "Tomorrow night is the M. House dance, I do hope it will not be too distressing for words. I am very cheered, for we are all going to eat and drink something at Tom's most cozy flat first and thus fortified, sail off to Montcrieff House on the courteous side of lateness." Fearing that the only drinks at the dance would be lemon fizz and lime juice cordial, my mother advised her colleagues to smuggle in a flask of alcohol. After one party she wrote, "The Montcrieff House party was not too bad, A little like the Palais de Dance at Blackpool in organisation, but the food sumptuous, drink flowing, the floor long and slippery and the rooms pretty. During the Paul Jones there was a constant screaming, "Ladies on the inside, Gents on the out! Carry on please etc you would have laughed. My 'Gents' were the only two worth dancing with, the rest were horrifying. The ladies slightly better."

On one occasion my mother wrote, "Montcrieff House is giving a Supper Dance on the 7th December, the new Secretary of M House does not think I exhibit the true house spirit, out of civility, asked a polite question about the party, she remarked with a triumphant leer that she hoped I realised it was a get together dance, and that all the girls would be coming (I suppose she thinks I have not got the free for all spirit of this age!) "Such fun, yes," I democratically replied with an inward groan of horror and a mental foresight of some of our more hectic ladies, particularly the housekeeper and the leader of the gang flinging their arms around the horrified neck of my most sensitive man, and of my demure girl being forced to throw one of her shoes into the middle of the room with joyful shrieks for that horribly coy shoe game. Anything might happen, and the responsibility is mine. Dear me!"

In one of my mother's letters home to my grandmother, written on October 25th 1944, she wrote of a tragic occasion when some of her colleagues had a houseboat party and the boat capsized and everyone on it was thrown into the Nile. Monica, one of her work colleagues, had been on the boat when it capsized. One person was killed, he was a great friend of Monica's and he died saving her life. My mother wrote, "It was all too terrible to go into. They got caught up in the electric wiring and he disentangled her and pushed her onto the land but slipped into the water himself. She also had to cope with his death and all the attendant horrors. It has been a great shock with awful complications including courts of inquiry and a wife in Italy. I have never seen people suffering from greater shock than they all were. Even the men look ghostly and distraught. One thing which is good is that Monica is crying and talking a lot which I encourage as it is much better than silent thinking. Why her devoted mother and stepfather who are in Cairo have not appeared or helped in any way I can't think. Monica says "poor Mother it has been a frightful shock for her." But all the same it seems most odd that Monica should be left at Montcrieff House and to roam around Cairo with her distracted houseboat friends. I can be of so little use as I am working most of the time, but I shall probably be able to take her to Palestine on leave later on. What I have seen today is that responsible people take charge of the legal side because for a future chief witness she is being very emotional and indiscreet and there are several complications. The office, bless them, are being sensible and helpful.

The other witnesses have rather melted away leaving Monica brandishing herself which is a pity."

At the time the British presence in Cairo was offensive to many Egyptians and therefore Britain was very keen to make sure that only positive news came from Egypt to England. It seems that no information on the houseboat tragedy and the ensuing court hearings was mentioned. Instead, news of the great cultural events such as Forces choir concerts in Cairo Cathedral was sent to London giving an impression of harmony between the British and the Egyptians.

My mother was very much a product of her class and generation. Born into an aristocratic family at a time of British imperialism, she was fiercely patriotic, young, passionate and ready to die for her country, unwavering in her beliefs of Empire. Many people were bitterly disillusioned by their class system that had led them into the horrors of the First World War. The economic pressure in the wake of the first war followed by the Second World War meant that many were questioning the old system and for many socialism seemed a better ideal with which to go forward. My mother's cousin, Charles Liddell, was based in Egypt fighting in the desert for six years, an experience which with every year that went by left him more disillusioned and questioning of the old world order and everything for which he was fighting. Increasingly in his letters, he described his despair with mankind, questioning his Christianity and starting to examine socialism as a way forward. It is clear from their correspondence that Pamela stuck firmly to the values of the old world with God on her side. In a letter to her dated 6/6/42 Charles wrote "If Christianity is to come to final victory, why are we bothering to fight, why aren't we all out preaching the word to Germans, Japanese and not minding a bit about the British Empire or what we eat or wear as long as we can live and die for Christ. If religion is as important to one as it says, surely then it is all that matters in life and death. Don't dismiss me as a stupid atheist. I am more a seeker after truth which at the moment I cannot find. Are the Germans being tested too? And can you really believe that God, who is our Father, engineers the horrors of this world. Test us by all means, but must babies be killed, children tortured women raped and men degraded to provide the examination paper."[25] He went on to say, " I believe that fundamentally undressed of all its clothing we are fighting for our existence, for our food, clothes and standard of living against the Germans who want to improve theirs, and our peace aims to try and create a world where those of us who live and our children won't have to do it again." Charles tried to persuade my mother to look forward, saying, "we must look to America as the next superpower, if this war ever ends".[26]

During the time of their correspondence, they discussed the big questions of war, empire, Christianity and how the European world of war could possibly rebuild itself and recover. Charles was much more ready for the new world of America as the next super power than my mother who went through a period of being angry with the Americans for not joining the war effort more quickly. Her time there did nothing to change her strong views. The correspondence between her and her cousin became passionate in their search for a sense of what really mattered going forward in time.

Charles described in his letters his nostalgia about their trips to Hayling Island in their youth. During his time in the desert, he wrote constantly of his wish for a bath, the constant heat and sand made him crave clean water.

When Charles heard that my mother was coming to Cairo he began to look forward to her arrival. In a letter to my mother dated 9th October 1943, he wrote: "You will find Cairo luxurious but frightfully expensive now and of course crowds of pleasure-seeking and rather sex-starved males, but all fairly easily dealt with I would say. Prices have risen a lot since I wrote to you."

Egypt during war time was such a distant world from Charles's and my mother's childhood memories of picnics and trips to Hayling Island to swim in the sea.

My mother wrote poems throughout her time in Egypt and used it as an outlet for so much emotion that could not otherwise be expressed. Her poems ranged from the despair of being sent away from her homeland into exile, to laments about having to share a communal house in Egypt.

She also wrote scathing verses about the tantrums of the women who sang in the Cairo Forces Cathedral Choir made up of British service men and women under the directorship of organist and choirmaster Clifford Harker. According to my mother the ladies were vying for Clifford's attention. Her poem 'The Choir' was published in *The Sphynx*, an English magazine published in Cairo, after which my mother was more than apprehensive about continuing to sing in the choir and fretted about the possible repercussions that might occur.

Cathedral Choir, Pamela 2nd row 5 in from the left
Above Cairo Cathedral Choir. Centre Conductor Clifford Harker.

Pamela front left, Clifford Harker 3rd from right.

Dress rehearsal for nativity play with carols.

The Choir decided to go to the Yugoslav Camp in the desert to put on an opera for the entertainment of refugees living in the camp.

In 1944 Yugoslavia was evacuated by the allies ahead of the German invasion. Yugoslav refugees lived there in tents until early 1946. Conditions in the desert were harsh and many of the children died. More than 30,000 people lived in the camp for 18 months after which they returned to Yugoslavia.

In December 1944 my mother wrote to her parents, "We have heard today that we

Choir setting off to put on opera for the Yugoslav Camp. Clifford bottom left, Sheila centre, Pamela top right.

are all to get forty-eight pounds back pay for the new rise (£70 per annum) in Foreign Service allowance. An astounding and very pleasing thought. I doubt I shall ever feel so rich again." She had previously lost an earring given to her by her father whilst riding a camel round the pyramids and now had enough money to go to a trinket shop in Cairo.

My mother remained working in 'A' Force Censorship in Cairo until 1945 when the war ended. In November 1944, she wrote to her father imploring him to ask 'The Big White Chief' (Sir Dick White, head of MI5) to summon her back to England. She made the point that she had already served double her time in the Middle East and had trained others to take her place. She wrote also that she would be of much more use in London. Her requests were ignored until the Censorship Department was closed at the end of the war and transferred to the Home Office in London. My mother and all her colleagues were then sent back to London. She went back to her family home, Dapplemere in Chorleywood, and took up work at the Home Office in London. She had been serving in Egypt for 18 months and was delighted to have the opportunity to return home.

In 1945 the Commander in Chief of the Middle East Postal Censorship, Colonel A. Saunders, awarded her a Commendation Card from the M.E.F General Orders 266 of 29/6/45 Mention in the Dispatches for "Outstandingly good services". My mother was an officer and a special sorter during her time in the Censorship Department in Egypt.

Once the Censorship Department was transferred back to London there was a celebration of its achievements in the Middle East. A high ranking official, Mr Locke, came to visit to congratulate them all on their achievements, in particular the discovery of top Nazi spy rings in America. From the photograph opposite of this party one can see how little food was on the table, a sign of the era of food rationing.

Postal and Telegraphic Censorship Department Special Sorters on first floor London. September 1945. Pamela centre back under the poster.

Pamela's dispatches certificate.

CHAPTER 6
Return to England: Temporary Peace

After the war, my mother worked for the Home Office in London. Having left Egypt as an Officer of the Postal and Telegraphic Censorship Department, which was largely dismantled, she had to find work in peacetime. She and all her colleagues had to be re-deployed. In 1945 MI5 was struggling to find direction. From 1945 onwards, it is unclear what Home Office work my mother was doing. It was a time of stagnation in British Intelligence. The allies had won the war against Hitler so there was no longer an obvious enemy, and the Soviet threat was in its infancy. So it seemed there was little to do at this time. She kept photographs, letters, and passports from her time during the war whilst serving in Bermuda and Egypt, all of these helped to build a clear picture of her life but from 1945 onwards there is much less information.

Now that she was back in England my mother was invited by the Royal Princesses Elizabeth and Margaret back to Buckingham Palace and Windsor Castle on a regular basis both to go to private parties at court and to sing with the princesses in the palace choir. The princesses invited her to their choir rehearsals every Thursday starting at 5.45 at the Palace and in Windsor Castle. She recorded these weekly gatherings in her 1945 and 1946 diaries.

In 1946 My mother was working for the Home Office in Victoria, London, and Robert, her father, was working in MI6 in Whitehall, They

Pamela back in cold blitzed England.

were partly living in 15 West Eaton Place so they no longer had to deal with a commute. In her diary on 20th September she wrote, "Poor Sheila in a sinister office – must get her out." 21st September, "Dad is going to get her out." Oct 1st "Sheila has filled out a form for a job in Daddy's Office Interview 2nd Oct 5.45." It is unclear what the sinister office was. A week later my grandfather had scooped Sheila out and put her to work elsewhere.

During this time my mother fell in love with my father, Charles Fane, who was a distant cousin. It is unclear exactly when the affair began but in

1946 my mother's uncle, Richard Cave, was a director of a shipping line and his wife Joan had been asked to launch a ship. My mother escorted her uncle and aunt and met Charles aboard the ship. According to my mother, it was love at first sight.

Pamela, ship's Captain, Joan Cave,
Pauline Fane, Charles Fane.

They also met each other socially with other family members. On 24th January 1946 my mother wrote in her diary that Charles and Pauline and their children came down for the day. On 29th May her diary record was "To Dine Pauline and Charles." On April 3rd she went to a Victory dance with Charles, Clifford Harker and a house party. The next day she wrote, "I wonder if I will ever hear from C again." Before long a love affair began, like her work the affair had to be a secret. My father will not have known about her work. By this time many levels of deception had woven their way into her life. As late as 1948 she was still singing with the princesses in Buckingham Palace who of course were also ignorant of the affair, which went on for years. Perhaps it suited her not to be married whilst working in MI5 because the service had a policy of not allowing its workers to marry at all and especially not divorcees. Charles also wanted to wait until his children were grown up before taking such a drastic step to divorce his wife. My mother adored her father Robert, whom she knew would not approve of the affair, therefore she could not bring herself to tell him about it. Robert died in 1964. MI5 Officers who intended to marry a divorcee were expected to resign from the service, however, that said, once working for MI5 one could not retire unless it was agreed by the service, and a person could not retire of their own free will. My mother told me as she was dying that she had been due for an O.B.E but she did not tell me that it was anything other than coincidence that at the age of 42, after years of being my father's mistress, she became pregnant with me and then married my father a year after I was born. My father had, by then, divorced his first wife. The scandal at the time was significant. My mother would not have been allowed to continue as an MI5 officer under those circumstances and aged 42 she wanted a chance of family life which had been denied her for so many years. She was very happy during the time that she was married to my father and certainly did not show any regret about her decision.

CHAPTER 7
Cold War and Betrayals

In 1950 my mother worked in 'B' section of MI5 which dealt with counter-espionage and was run by Sir Dick White. In 1951 she wrote to
a publisher of poetry a short description of her post-war life saying,
"Since the war I have worked in the War Office, done the London debutante season, attended some private parties at court and canvassed in
Fulham during the last election." She also worked as a volunteer in the
National Adoption Society, which, pre contraception in the '50s, was a
much needed organisation.

In 1953 there was a reorganisation of MI5. Sir Dick White was made
the Director General and counter-intelligence moved to 'D' section run by
Graham Mitchell. In 1956 Roger Hollis became the Director General and
remained so until after my mother retired.

My mother's new job in MI5 took her in a very different direction to
post-war work in the War Office. The next fifteen years would be work
almost entirely dedicated to fighting the threat of communism from
Soviet Russia. MI5 was also watching the activities of the Trades Unions
in the United Kingdom. Whilst working in MI5 my mother had access
to a 'black list' of people who were considered to be communist sympa-
thisers and, much to her astonishment, she saw one of her aunt's name
on the list. The aunt in question was thought to be spending time with
Robert Maxwell, a Czechoslovakian immigrant with socialist politics.

My mother tried to deter her aunt without giving away the source of her information.

Shelagh Comyns, a family friend, wrote about my mother in 1954, "Pamela is unmarried at present and works at the War Office. She, like her ancient cousin, writes poetry in her spare time and has a voice like a nightingale as the name Synge would lead you to believe."[27]

Volkov and 'The Cambridge Five'

In 1945 a Russian called Konstantin Volkov walked into the British Embassy in Turkey. He said he was a NKVD officer and wished to defect to the West. In return he said he would give the names of three Soviet agents working in Britain in our intelligence services, two in MI6 (now known to have been Guy Burgess and Donald Maclean) and one in the Counter Intelligence Section in the British Secret Service (now known to have been Kim Philby). Volkov also offered to give names of many more Soviet agents working in Britain and Turkey. As Philby was in the intelligence section he managed to tip off the Soviets about Volkov's wish to defect. Within no time Volkov was put on a plane to Russia and was not heard of again. The affair did however start the investigation into Burgess, Maclean and Philby that eventually led to their own uncovering and eventual defections to Russia. After Volkov's statement my mother was put in a team under the guidance of Guy Liddell to put some physical and phone surveillance on a list of nine British intelligence officers suspected of spying for the Russians. Kim Philby, Guy Burgess, Donald Maclean, Anthony Blunt and John Cairncross were all on the list. According to Chapman Pincher when interviewed by me in 2006, "The early suspicion of Blunt (whose code-name on the list of nine was Blunden) is also contrary to the official story, which claimed that he had never been suspect until his friend Burgess had defected. Pam Synge, who took part in the telephone tapping, told me that all that resulted from the surveillance of Blunt was disclosure of his unsavoury private life with 'rough trade' so he was struck from the list."

Kim Philby, Guy Burgess, Donald Maclean, Anthony Blunt and John Cairncross were all Englishmen who went to Cambridge University in the

1930s and were all turned to support communism and the Soviet Union during their time at Cambridge. They are now generally referred to as 'The Cambridge Five.' They soon became convinced that the world needed communism to counteract the rising threat of fascism. Philby founded the group and recruited Burgess who then recruited Blunt. Both Burgess and Blunt were bisexual but became increasingly homosexual. Maclean was married but was also bisexual at a time when it was illegal to be homosexual. The bond between them all was immensely strong. Cairncross did not grow up with the same privileges as the other four men and did not form a close bond with any of them. According to David Leitch in his introduction to Yuri Modin's *My Five Cambridge Friends*, "These likely and oh so bright lads from Cambridge constituted the most influential spy-ring of the first half of the century, and probably all time." [28] Having been tipped off by Philby that their cover had been blown, Burgess and Maclean fled to Moscow into a life of exile in 1951. Philby was not exposed until 1964 when he also fled to Moscow. Cairncross escaped prosecution and was not uncovered until the 1970's.

As early as 1940 Cairncross informed Moscow that the Americans and the British had been working on the joint manufacture of an atomic bomb, giving the Russians enough technical information to enable them to make their own.

By 1944 Philby had worked his way up in the Secret Service. Astonishingly, being a Soviet agent, he "had become head of the section within British Intelligence whose sole mission was to do battle with the KGB and thwart the spread of Communism worldwide." [29]

Blunt, Burgess, Maclean and Philby believed that communism was the ideology to fight for, even when Russia was not living up to the ideal. None of them wished to live in Russia and made that abundantly clear after visiting the country.

After their defections, and living in exile, Philby and Burgess refused to learn Russian but Maclean studied Russian and according to Yuri Modin, became fluent. Philby ordered marmalade and books to be sent from England and had everything he needed provided by the KGB but refused to see Burgess: he felt betrayed by his old friend and fellow conspirator, because he had defected with Maclean leaving him (Philby) vulnerable to being found out as a Soviet spy. Burgess, who still managed to get suits made by his tailor in London, was very unhappy, relying heavily on alcohol, and died in 1963 at the age of 52, a year before my mother left the service.

In 1964, as my mother was leaving the service, Blunt confessed to working for the Russians in return for a deal not to prosecute him. He was a third cousin of the Queen Mother, the Queen's art advisor and a leading British art historian. He had received a knighthood from the Queen. The embarrassment that someone so close to the Crown could be a Soviet spy was so great that no one wanted the public to know, including the Royal Court, so he was offered immunity from prosecution. Eventually, in 1979 Blunt was exposed by the Prime Minister Margaret Thatcher in the House of Commons. Cairncross also confessed in 1964 but there was not enough evidence to prosecute him. As Burgess, Maclean and Philby had all fled to Russia, not one of the spy ring were prosecuted.

None of the five men regretted the course they took, they all remained committed communists and none of them did it for money. At one point the KGB was so grateful to them that they offered payment. All of them refused to take it until they were living in exile in Russia and therefore had little choice. The core of their belief was that only communism could save the world. After the First World War and the depression that followed, the capitalist countries were in economic as well as political trouble. In the book *Conspiracy of Silence: the Secret Life of Anthony Blunt*, Barrie Penrose and Simon Freeman wrote, "In the general election of May 1929 the Labour Party, led by Ramsay Macdonald, had defeated the Conservatives. But Labour seemed just as bewildered as its political opponents. Capitalism, which had always been seen as self-regulating, appeared to be on the point of collapse; a view that was reinforced when the motor of the world economy, the American Stock Exchange on Wall Street, crashed."[30]

The financial depression that followed was felt across the world and combined with the fact that Nazism and antisemitism was on the rise caused many to join the Communist Party in Great Britain as it was seen as the only way to fight off the Nazi regime.

Penrose and Freeman went on to write about the rise of the fascist, Oswald Mosley, in Britain, "but then Mosley, who had appeared to many to be simply bringing a radical but patriotic approach to politics, became openly antisemitic and Hitlerite. Many supporters dropped out, to be replaced by thugs who liked the idea of beating up Jews. There is no doubt that the rise of the Blackshirts helped the communists."[31]

Whilst Blunt and Philby were reporting to Moscow from MI5 and MI6 my mother was involved with monitoring the rise of the British Communist Party and the trades unions, watching their influence on British politics. Olive Synge, her sister-in-law, worked with her briefly in MI5 and said that they were in separate rooms listening to taped phone conversations on intercepts recorded at 75 rpm. Olive never knew what my mother was up to but said that the room she was in had much more action than hers and that she would often disappear on an operation. She was also of the impression that the work that my mother did in Cairo was more interesting than what she was doing in London: listening to endless intercepts in damp London, Olive thought, must have been less colourful than life in Egypt.

Olive went on to say that in London my mother was in charge of a safe house where MI5 were protecting a Russian army deserter in a flat in North London. Whilst Olive was temporarily in charge the Russian asked if he could go out to buy some cigarettes and she agreed that he could. Outside he bumped into a fellow Russian who invited him for a drink. He turned out to be a KGB agent, and the deserter was never seen again. Olive felt the burden of that guilt for the rest of her life. Olive had to leave MI5 because she suffered badly from asthma which the equipment they used set off.

In the 1950's my mother was mainly working for MI5. Olive described how my mother would get theatre tickets for trade union bosses and her colleagues would then raid their houses whilst they were at the theatre. In 1955 my mother was part of a team that organised something called

'Operation Party Piece'. MI5 were attempting to infiltrate the British Communist Party so they effectively burgled a flat in Mayfair which was the British headquarters of the Communist Party and over a two month period copied 55,000 membership files contained there. With that information my mother and her colleagues could monitor the movements of individuals of interest who were now known to be members of the Party. In my interview with Chapman Pincher in 2006 I told him that my mother was involved with British politics and trades unions, his response was: "Well that would make sense because they tended to use women for trade union business." He went on to say: "they would get theatre tickets for these chaps and then they would go in, they would decide that they wanted to see inside someone's flat, they would do a lot of research and find out where this fellow was from and they would choose, if possible, a time when he was on holiday."[32]

A female colleague of my mother in MI5 described the hierarchy of the office in the '50s. The higher the floor that officers worked on the greater their importance. The telephone tappers were on the 6th floor so my mother would have spent time there. Her colleague said that she worked on a lower floor. She recalled that there was a terrifying female boss called Millicent Bagot known amongst the secretaries as 'The Bag'. Bagot was one of the first females in the Security Service to reach senior rank. On one occasion my mother's colleague took some files up to the 5th floor and, when the lift door opened there stood a furious Miss Bagot who sent her back down to her correct floor saying that she must never come up to the higher floors again. Suitably chastised, she did not venture up again. My mother would almost certainly have worked under Bagot as she was an expert on Soviet Communism and was one of the first people in MI5 to raise the alarm about Kim Philby being a Soviet agent.

In 1951 Philby received information that Donald Maclean was suspected as a Soviet spy and told Guy Burgess to warn him. The KGB ordered Burgess to escort Maclean to Russia, fearing that Maclean would not defect on his own and could break down under pressure. Burgess escorted him thinking that once Maclean was delivered safely he could return to England but he was never able to return. Maclean and Burgess' sudden disappearance sent shock waves through Great Britain and the United States. We were working closely with the Americans, not only on the atomic programme but also in the fight against communism.

My mother was part of a team under Sir Dick White who tried to stop Burgess and Maclean from defecting to Russia. She recounted to Pincher years later that every time she tried to get anything done to stop them from defecting, " a cold hand came down from above" which stopped any action from taking place. MI5 maintained that they were unaware that Burgess was a spy before his defection. Chapman Pincher referred to my mother as one of two prime witnesses who stated that that was not true. In his book *Treachery*, Pincher wrote: "According to Pamela Synge, a member of MI5 who was involved with the saga, one of the first actions after receiving news that 'Homer' was probably British was an examination of the document that had been submitted by the would-be KGB defector Konstantin Volkov. It was seen that Volkov had offered to give leads to seven Soviet agents, five in British intelligence and two in the Foreign Office. Under the guidance of Guy Liddell, nine possible suspects were selected, and they were all put under some degree of physical and telephone surveillance for several weeks."[33] Guy Burgess, code name 'Homer', was on that list of nine suspected Soviet agents.

In 1985 Chapman Pincher wrote to my mother to see if, with hindsight she could throw any more light on the subject of the Soviet agents working in our intelligence services in the '50s.

There have been many theories that Roger Hollis, head of MI5 at the time, was actually a Russian spy working as head of British intelligence, Pincher spent years trying to prove that this was the case and wrote many books to back up his theory. He died as information was becoming more available due to the 50 year Freedom of Information Act, and it is now generally accepted that Hollis was not working for the Russians. My mother did not live long enough to know that, however. The cloud of suspicion fell on so many causing a high level of anxiety and paranoia within the service. In 1951 my mother and her colleagues and my grandfather, Robert, knew

BUSINESS : 0488 58855
PRIVATE : 0488 58397

CHURCH HOUSE
16, CHURCH STREET
KINTBURY
NEWBURY
BERKSHIRE RG15 0TR

8th November 1985

Dear Pam,

I hope that you enjoyed your holiday in America and have returned refreshed.

Have you managed to wade through any more of the book? If so has it jogged your memory in any way or have you any comments?

I have not made any progress with my researches to date on the question of the List of Nine. I wondered if, in fact, you had managed to find any of your former colleagues who confirm that it did exist before the M and B defection. I am still extremely interested to establish the existence of this list.

You have confirmed your recollection that Philby's code-name in the inquiries was PEACH. Does ORANGE ring a bell for Burgess? Or any other fruit?

It would be a pleasure to see you again. Could I come over again at some convenient time soon?

Best wishes,

Yours sincerely,

C.P.

that Philby was working for the Soviets from within MI6 but they could not get enough proof to do anything about it and he was very clever at handling questions about his activities. He even went as far as giving a press conference to try and protest his innocence, but the disappearance of Burgess and Maclean threw too much suspicion on Philby.

Years later my mother's brother, Allen, wrote a letter to me titled *Spies*. In the letter he wrote, "a sociable neighbour had called round at our house to announce the arrival in the neighbourhood of a charming couple called the Kim Philbys. She felt my father Robert must know him as a fellow Foreign Office man and she suggested meeting over cocktails. I noticed at this point that my father had turned green, as he had once turned green over a plate of boiled squid in France. At the same time my sister Pam, who worked for MI5 was looking with furrowed brows at the carpet."[34]

The village where they lived was Chorleywood. The 'new couple' had moved to Heronsgate, and by pure chance the cottage was a mile and a half away from my grandfather's house, this was shortly after Philby was considered a suspect and had resigned from MI6.

It was 1951 and Philby had been paid off by MI6 as he was, by this time, considered guilty by many. Allen also wrote, "The good neighbour had one question about the new arrivals she thought Robert might be able to resolve. The Philbys' bed clothes could be spied lying on the lawn of an early morning. After the neighbour left Pam whispered, " Oh God he is one of them, even Skardon couldn't break him down". Allen Synge *Spies*.[35]

Skardon was a brilliant special branch officer who became an MI5 interrogator, and had a reputation for successfully getting spies to confess. He interrogated Philby ten times but failed to get a confession out of him. As the service and the American service became increasingly suspicious, Philby decided to defect to Russia in 1963.

Anthony Blunt was also on the list of suspected Soviet spies working in MI5 and MI6. In his book *Treachery*, Pincher wrote, "The early suspicion of Blunt (whose code name on the List of Nine was 'Blunden') is also contrary to the official story, which claimed that he had never been suspect until after his friend Burgess had defected. Pam Synge, who took part in the phone tapping, told me that all that resulted from the surveillance of Blunt was disclosure of his unsavoury private life with 'rough trade,' so he was struck from the list."[36]

What would have seemed inconceivable was that the privileged young men who worked for British intelligence could turn on their own class and country towards the ideal of communism. At the time it was not considered possible that the world famous Cambridge University could have Soviet recruiters working as lecturers. To have made such an investigation would have been "nothing less than an investigation in to Britain's ruling class."[37]

Sir Dick White later admitted that it was a mistake that they had failed to monitor British universities. Evidence in letters found in Burgess's home showed that he and his fellow Cambridge students, Burgess, Maclean and Philby, had been turned during their time there. Educated at the country's top public schools and enjoying a life of privilege, it did not seem possible that they could follow an ideology of communism which was so far apart from their world of comfort and their place in, as it was seen, the ruling class, to the extent that they would betray their country and put themselves in danger in order to do so. My mother was in an uncomfortable position spying on colleagues who were from the same background as she was. It would have deeply shaken her. It is clear that during her service during the war she felt she was fighting for country, empire and the existing class system, only to find that the traitors were from the elite class in which she believed and of which she was a part.

In later years I never understood her aversion to intellectuals and if I showed any intellectual curiosity about the world she would say, "Darling are you reading too many strange books in your attic?" She was appalled at the prospect of having a blue stocking daughter and as I was reading Virginia Woolf at the time, this seemed to be conclusive evidence that I was heading that way, especially as she did not approve of the Bloomsbury set due to their appetite for gay sex and their liberal attitudes. Now I understand her fears a bit better. All her bosses who turned out to be Soviet spies were intellectuals who believed in the ideology of communism and many had been turned during their time at university. She had to watch the British Intelligence Service, to which she had devoted twenty-four years of her adult life, being turned upside down by constant revelations of Soviet spies working in the institution. A strong belief system in the old world order was publicly and privately turned upside down. Even her cousin Guy Liddell who became Director General of MI5 was briefly suspected as 'the fifth man' of the spy ring. He had been close to Philby, Burgess and Anthony Blunt. Liddell was finally cleared of suspicion three years after my mother's death in 1990 when John Cairncross was found to be the fifth man. My mother, like many in her field, went to her death not knowing who, in our intelligence services, were and who were not spying for the Russians.

David Mure in his book, *Master of Deception: Tangled Webs in London and the Middle East*, wrote on the subject of the intellectuals who were turned, "I believe that many of the seeds of this decay may be found in the kind of people, mostly intellectuals, who were recruited into the war time Intelligence Services and whose power for harm was enormously increased by the lack of control over individual decisions surviving from the Victorian era. Then the establishment was governed by a code, narrow and restrictive, certainly, but in its reliance on absolute integrity probably the highest expression yet of Christian civilisation".[38]. Mure goes on to say, "When in the twentieth century this code was penetrated by odious and disloyal ideas, still I am sure an anathema to the vast majority of Englishmen, what had formerly been a strength became a deadly danger."[39]

Mure also wrote about Blunt, Burgess, Philby and other turned Englishmen, "Unfortunately, some of their consciences whilst clear that the Allies must win the war were equally clear that the Soviets should win the peace. Therefore there is little question that Blunt's conscience would have told him that his duty was plain, to tell all he knew to his Russian Controller."[40]

According to Mure, there were many more Soviet agents working in MI5 than MI6. A message received from Colonel Wild, Head of 'Ops' 'B' G3 Division SHAEF from 1944-1945, stated:

"The discussions on how to present the ineptitude of 'B' Division MI5 have called to my mind the appearance of Anthony Blunt as liaison officer between that Division and Ops 'B'. This appointment demonstrates as nothing else does the Soviet penetration of MI5."

Mure wrote of Blunt, "I just couldn't see how, even in the wonderful world of MI5, an aesthete who had never heard a shot fired, let alone in anger, and had been dismissed from his only Staff course on security grounds could have been chosen for a specialist operational job."[41]

Blunt and my mother were both distantly related to the Queen Mother. I do not know, when she was phone tapping him and watching him, whether she knew this. Her cousin, Guy Liddell, was deputy head of MI5 and as already mentioned was at one point under suspicion of being a Soviet spy due to his close relationship with Blunt. For my mother it was not only her class who were betraying their country but also, seemingly, her relatives as well.

CHAPTER 8
Commander Crabb Disappearance

On June 9th 1957, a corpse floating in Chichester Harbour was spotted by two fishermen. It was headless, had no hands and most of the upper body was eaten by fish but the lower part of his body was preserved by a diving suit. Police believed it was the body of Lionel Crabb, a fearless military diver who, on 19th April 1956, went for his last dive and never returned. There are several complex and conflicting conspiracy theories as to what happened to Crabb, the most popular theory at the time was that he had been captured and brainwashed and was working for the Russian navy. The British security service still considers the subject so sensitive that none of the files on Crabb will be released until 2057.

Crabb was considered a hero and was awarded the George Medal for removing limpet mines from ships' hulls in Gibraltar Harbour by fighting Italian frogmen during the Second World War. He also dismantled unexploded German torpedoes and booby-trapped ships in Venice and was made an OBE. In 1955 he was enlisted by MI5 to examine Soviet ships' hulls.

On April 18th 1956 the Russian President Khruschev came to Portsmouth on the Russian warship *Ordzhonikidze*, with the purpose of his visit being to have talks with the British Prime Minister, Anthony Eden. As it was deemed a peaceful visit Eden told MI5 not to allow any of our divers to dive under the Russian ship. His instructions were ignored.

Shortly before he disappeared Crabb received a letter from the Admiralty which ended with this: "Because of the present general position... there is no possibility of your being asked to extend your naval service beyond the current period."[42] There was no pension as he had been a reserve officer.

50 years later his former diving partner and friend Sydney Knowles gave an interview to Tim Binding who was writing a fictional account of Crabb's life, *Man Overboard*. Knowles, now in his 80s and living in Australia claimed that Crabb was murdered by MI5 and that an unknown diver was sent with Crabb on that last dive. Knowles said that Crabb had been a friend of Anthony Blunt and he had accompanied Crabb to dinners with lots of young men where Blunt was frequently involved. Knowles was amazed by "the homosexual nature of the gathering and the political overtones – the talk of the glories of Communism and the Soviet Union."[43] Crabb had apparently told Knowles that he was considering defecting to Russia for the diving opportunities. Knowles told Binding that MI5 knew that Crabb was intending to defect to the USSR and had arranged the mission under the *Ordzhonikidze* specifically to have him eliminated.[44]

The reason that Knowles was certain MI5 knew that Crabb was intending to defect was because Knowles had, anonymously, tipped them off himself.

The Prime Minister, Eden, was furious that his orders not to authorise any diving had been ignored. MI5 tried to deny any knowledge of the dive. However, my mother was working in MI5, 'A' division at the time under the administration of Malcolm Cumming. Chapman Pincher, who interviewed my mother on the matter wrote, "An MI5 member, Pam Synge, was later to describe to me how Malcolm Cummings had told her, with almost schoolboy excitement, 'Crabb is going under that Russian warship in the morning!'"[45]

In 2007, a retired Russian frogman, Eduard Koltsov, claimed to have cut Crabb's throat after catching him placing a mine on the *Ordzhonikidze* whilst it was in Portsmouth Harbour.

A still secret report of an Admiralty Board of Inquiry into the cause of Crabb's death had concluded that because of strong tides and being weighted, he had become trapped in the underwater timbers of a jetty, where he had run out of oxygen.[46]

According to Dan Hale who wrote a book about Crabb called *The Final Dive*, "When the diver's body was first found, Crabb's fiancée Pat Rose was adamant that it wasn't Lionel Crabb."[47] Hale went on to write, "To her final days Pat Rose remained convinced that Lionel's death was faked. Pat used to tell family members: 'We will soon be together. He has been training Russian frogmen in the Black Sea.'"[48]

Whatever happened on the morning of his disappearance, the Security Service could not face the possibility of yet another defection to Soviet Russia of one of our British heroes so any other outcome would have been preferential. His disappearance has been considered one of the most enduring mysteries of the Cold War.

Crabb worked under Ian Fleming during the Second World War at Naval Intelligence and Fleming later used Crabb as his inspiration for his 'James Bond' novels.[49]

As children, my mother banned us from watching James Bond films because she considered them to be 'decadent'. The only chance we had of watching them was if our uncle Allen was staying whilst a Bond film was on. We could hide behind the sofa and watch bits of the film when my mother was not in the room. Perhaps the films were too close to the bone, or maybe so far from the real atmosphere in the Intelligence Services, that they made her angry, either way the real life antics of our Intelligence Services, the Russian Intelligence Services, the CIA, FBI and the German Abwehr all show both how creative and destructive humans become when at war.

Conclusion

After a twenty-four year career and after a long affair with my father Charles, my mother became pregnant with me at the age of 42 and so she retired from the service.

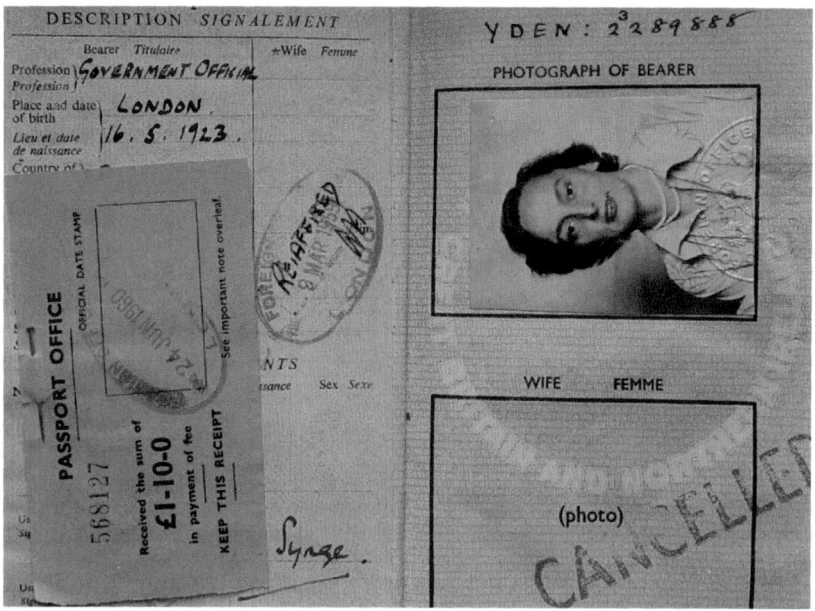

After a painful divorce my father married my mother a year later and they bought a manor house in the countryside and moved out of London. My mother went on to safely deliver my two sisters.

I remember my father as an austere distant figure. He employed an army of nannies to keep us all in hand at all times. My mother was deeply in love with him and they enjoyed a full and vibrant life together.

On March 15th 1976, my mother went to the village post office to buy some stamps. When she got home she found my father dead. In her absence he had suffered a fatal heart attack. It was a brutal shock for us all but especially my mother. I was eleven and my sisters were eight and nine years old. I was sent to boarding school straight away. Six months later my mother was diagnosed with breast cancer. As she had three daughters to get to adulthood

Pamela with my father Charles Fane 1960's.

she decided that she would live until the youngest was eighteen. She succeeded despite the odds and was courageous all the way through.

My mother entertaining my friends at my 21st birthday party shortly before she died.

When she was dying the local vicar came to see her to tell her that Jesus was waiting for her on the other side. Her response was, "That is frightfully kind of him but would you please tell him I am not ready to meet him yet." She died aged sixty-four in 1987.

On the day of her funeral one of the children from the village came running towards me waving a letter shouting, "It's from the Queen", a letter of condolence. On my mother's gravestone my sisters and I had engraved "The golden thread of courage has no end" which we felt was a fitting epitaph.[50]

Although she is no longer with us this book will on some level posthumously give my mother a voice and tell some of the story she was forbidden to tell.

Endnotes

1 *Traitors*, Chapman Pincher (1987).
2 *The Talking Book,* Allen Synge
3 Belstead School Aldeburgh. oneplacestudy.org/Belstead House
4 *The Little Princesses: The story of the Queen's childhood by her nanny,* Marion Crawford (2003).
5 *Royal Guides: A Story of the 1st Buckingham Palace Company,* V.M. Synge (1948) – The beginnings, p 11
6 *Ibid.* An Evacuee Company, p 32
7 *Ibid.* p 34
8 *Ibid.* we turn Commando, p 42
9 *What was the Blitz? Britain since the 1930s* eworkhelp.co.uk
10 *The Evacuees*, edited by B.S. Johnson, Gollancz (1968) – Allen Synge, p 253
11 *Ibid.* – Allen Synge p 258, an extract from the novel, *The Evacuation of Edward*
12 Allen Synge *The Talking Book*
13 *Ibid*
14 *The Evacuees*, edited by B.S. Johnson, Gollancz (1968)
15 From a poem by Pamela Synge
16 *Bernews* October 14 2019 – Wartime Spies who read the mail in Bermuda
17 Bermuda-online.org
18 Bermuda-online.org history 1939-1951
19 *Cairo in the War: 1939-1945*, Artemis Cooper, John Murray (2013) –Prologue, p 6
20 *Ibid.* – Prologue p 4
21 *Master of deception: Tangled webs in London and the Middle East,* David Mure, William Kimber (1980) – p 96.
22 *Ibid.* – p 84
23 *Cairo Child*, Pamela Ormerod, Sphinx Press (2004) – p 133

24 National archives Cairo DEFE1 Overseas Censorship

25 Letter to Pamela from Charles Liddell written 06/06/42

26 Letter to Pamela from Charles Liddell written 06/06/42

27 Description by Shelagh Comyns, a family friend 29.4.1954.

28 David Leitch, p 3 in his introduction to *My Five Cambridge Friends*, Yuri Modin, Headline (1994).

29 *Ibid*, p122

30 *Conspiracy* of Silence: the secret life of Anthony Blunt, Barrie Penrose and Simon Freeman, Grafton Books (1986) – The Secret Apostles, p 75.

31 *Ibid.* – Radical Young Gentlemen, p 104.

32 Personal interview with Chapman Pincher 26/02/2006

33 *Treachery: Betrayals, Blunders, and Cover-ups: Six Decades of Espionage Against America and Great Britain*, Chapman Pincher Random House (2009) – Chapter 54, A List of Nine, p 386

34 Allen Synge letter to Eleanor Fane *Spies*.

35 *Ibid.*

36 *Treachery: Betrayals, Blunders, and Cover-ups: Six Decades of Espionage Against America and Great Britain*, Chapman Pincher – Chapter 54, A List of Nine, p 386

37 *The Perfect English Spy: Sir Dick White and the Secret War 1935-90*, Tom Bower, St Martin's Press New York (1995).

38 *Master of Deception: Tangled Webs in London and the Middle East*, David Mure, William Kimber (1980) – The World's Worst Staff Work, p 180

39 *Ibid.* – Afterword, p 262

40 *Ibid*

41 *Ibid*

42 *Frogman: Commander Crabb's Story*, Marshall Pugh, Charles Scribner (1956) – Chapter14, Last Dive p 191

43 *The Mail on Sunday March* 26 2006, article by Tim Binding, p 53

44 *Plymouth Herald*, 'Headless Body Found after Royal Navy Hero Vanished while Spying on Russians.' On the anniversary of his inquest in 1957.

45 *Treachery: Betrayals, Blunders, and cover ups: Six decades of Espionage Against America and Great Britain*, Chapman Pincher, Random House (2009) – A Ruthless Defamation, p 423.

46 *Ibid.* – p 422.

47 *Ian Fleming's Favourite Spy: Buster Crabb, Don Hale*, The History Press (2020) – Body of evidence, p 321.

48 *Ibid.* – p 422

49 thehistorypress.co.uk/articles/buster-crabb-ian-fleming-s-favorite-spy

50 Taken from a poem by Rowan Story.

Notes

Nicknames

Pamela and her family gave each other and their friends colourful nicknames. I had to do a certain amount of detective work to work them out. In writing this book I have had wonderful moments driving my children to school or sitting on a train platform, when suddenly I would connect a nickname with a person. In one of her letters from Cairo, Pamela writes to her father, "Daddy you really must write to the 'Big White Chief' and ask if I can come back." I kept thinking 'White????' Then the penny dropped – of course, Sir Dick White, head of MI5.

Dishcloth, Spiech, Wormy, Big White Chief, Lady Hanka Manka, aging aunt.

Notes and Sources

MEF certificate photo
photograph taken for American Vogue by Prince Fahreddin of Turkey

Acknowledgments

I would like to express my grateful thanks to Harry Chapman Pincher for all the time and knowledge he shared with me. I would like to thank his children Michael and Pat for granting permission for the publishing of two of their father's letters.

Bibliography

Bower, Tom, *The Perfect English Spy*, St. Martin's Press (1995), The unknown man in charge during the most tumultuous, scandal-ridden era in espionage history.

Cooper, *Artemis, Cairo In The War: 1939-1945*, John Murray (2013).

Crawford, Marion, The Little Princesses, Orion Books (2003).

Hale, Don, *Ian Fleming's Favourite Spy: Buster Crabb*, The History Press (2020).

Johnson, B.S., *The Evacuees*, Gollancz (1968).

Modin, Yuri, *My Five Cambridge Friends: Burgess, Maclean, Philby, Blunt and Cairncross: by their KGB Controller*, Headline (1994).

Mure, David, *Master of Deception: Tangled Webs in London and the Middle East*, William Kimber (1980).

Ormerod, Paula, *Cairo Child*, Sphinx Press (2004).

Penrose, Barrie and Freeman, Simon, *Conspiracy Of Silence: the Secret Life of Anthony Blunt*, Grafton Books, (1986).

Pincher, Chapman, *Treachery: Betrayals, Blunders, and Cover-ups: Six Decades of Espionage Against America and Great Britain*, Random House (2009).

Pugh, Marshall, *Frogman: Commander Crabb's Story*, Charles Scribner (1956).

Synge, Allen *The talking book.*

Synge, V.M., *Royal Guides The Girl Guides Association* (1948).

Index

About the Author

Eleanor Fane studied Russian and European Studies, which included Twentieth century European history and Literature from 1991-1995 at Queen Mary and Westfield College, London University.